Sanctum of Shadows
Volume I: The Satanist

Aleister Nacht

Sanctum of Shadows

© 2013 Aleister Nacht

Published by Loki/Speckbohne Publishing

ISBN-10: 0985707070

ISBN-13: 978-0985707071

First Edition

10 9 8 7 6 5 4 3 2 1

Printed in the United States of America

Sanctum of Shadows

Connect with Aleister Nacht on the World Wide Web:

Aleister Nacht's Website
www.AleisterNacht.com

Aleister Nacht's Blog
www.SatanicMagic.org

Satanic Magic Blog
www.SatanicMagic.Wordpress.com

Loki / Speckbohne Publishing
www.LokiSpeckbohne.com

Sanctum of Shadows

Table of Contents

Preface to Higher Magic 2

Satanism 16

Demoniac 24

Ascendancy 30

Inexorable 36

Finsteres Schloß 44

Sympathetic Magic 56

Die Rohe Unkontrollierte Magie 70

Verständlich 78

Kaltblütig 88

Beholder 94

Chakras 102

The Warrior 124

The Coven 128

Silentium In Persona Diaboli 136

Wichtige Absätze 142

Vampirism 154

Advice 168

In Closing 174

Glossary 176

Preface to Higher Magic

"Words are the tools that build ideas." Aleister Nacht

Satan, come into our hearts and come into our midst

Bless our unholy coven and bless those seeking truth

Your justice will be shown and will bless them

Bless our Satanic works; be with us Father Satan

We call upon you for your help and guidance

Hear our words, Satan hear our cries

As we place a sacrifice upon your altar

Hail Satan!

The change of reality is sometimes difficult for new Satanists to accept. Perhaps the new Devotee is carrying a huge amount of psychological baggage from the past and simply cannot (or will not) offload the burden. Whether self-inflicted or burnt into the psyche as a hot iron, these things of the past must remain in the past.

We all have scars (inside and outside) that hurt from time to time. A person need not be ashamed of the scars after all, they are a part of us and are as unique as the individual. Before you find the solution, you must first know the problem. So what seems to be 'your' problem?

Anyone selling a book that claims to answer all of the questions about Satanic Magic is certainly selling you a book of lies. Look beyond yourself and consider what is suggested herein; search deep in your heart to recognize your strengths and weaknesses.

Learning to be a Satanist is as much about learning *who you are* as it is learning magical operations and practices. You will not, I repeat, you will not master magic without knowing who you are and your personal limitations. If you do not know what your limits are, you will never know if you have exceeded those limits.

The first volume is written as a building block for the entire "Sanctum of Shadows" collection. These volumes represent an intellectual guide to development of the Satanic Higher Magic processes. Each volume concentrates on the in-depth analysis of the particular element that leads to Higher Magic study and practice.

I will not lead you astray however, I will say these techniques have consistently worked for me over the span of over twenty-five years. I wish to share these ideas and techniques with you and no other promises will be made. I believe that if you *diligently practice* these techniques, you will be successful in your pursuit of Satanic Magic mastery.

I am at the age in life where I do not want to *debate* or "prove" anything to anyone. If you do not believe in Satan, stop reading now and start a bonfire with this book. If you are so convinced that atheists are right in their belief, no one can help (or teach) you anything. I really do not care if you believe me or not......I know the truth and that is all that matters to me.

Satan is not going to appear "at your command" nor will your petty sniveling cause demons to appear to "prove" their existence. Satan and demons are much more advanced than humans, yet many people want to believe they can be controlled like a trained animal. Graveyards and mental hospitals are full of those idiots who thought they were so much smarter than anyone; including Satan. After all, if Satan does not exist as the atheists claim, why are they so fascinated with Him?

You will learn techniques and methodologies in this book that you may find useful. The methodologies, techniques and applications are over 20 years old. I have experimented with all of these practices throughout my entire adult life; beginning many, many years ago as a teenager.

In the practice of Satanism, certain things work and certain things do not work. You will find a healthy balance between the two however, you will not find **all** of the answers to your questions as such. A Satanist must be open-minded and must believe some of those things that may sound totally *unbelievable*. It is for that reason, many people do not grasp the true potential of Satanic Magic.

From the very young and tender age, when told Santa Claus does not exist or perhaps the Easter bunny does not exist, individuals have formulated their own reality of their physical world. That reality will work against the Satanist if allowed to take root in the person's psyche.

The book you hold your hand has true Satanic Power. The knowledge skills and abilities are going to be left totally up to you. This book will give you direction; it will give you guidance and perhaps also trigger fertile ideas. This book will not tell you how to become a magician and it will certainly not tell you how to become a Satanic Magus. Perhaps that will be a future book.

Some topics would fill several lengthy textbooks and are not easily discussed or applicable questions answered. I personally provide such training to those members of our coven because the complexity of the subject matter is better adapted to one-on-one teaching / mentoring. It is a deep and wide chasm to bridge.

This book will guide you to certain realizations and realities but it will be up to you to follow up and grasp those tidbits and elements of Satanic Magic. Proceed with the rest of this book at your own risk for there is a peril and there are consequences involved if treated with impunity. The Black Flame most certainly will burn you.

If I can speak to your innermost *"Magical Being"* then I will feel like my task has been accomplished. I will not leave you *high and dry* when it comes to such culpability however, as I mention in my other books, I will not cater to incompetence and "dumb-down" the Satanic message. I expect all Satanists to be intelligent, open-minded and resourceful individuals. Satanists will invest the time and energy required and Satanists certainly will not be fooled by *"smoke and mirrors"*. For the atheist, this Satanic gate is better remaining closed and locked.

It is also important to realize Satanism is not a club, social status or "equal opportunity" philosophy. Those who invest their time and energy may or may not achieve the reward. Cognitive and natural abilities are different for everyone. This is a determining factor for future success. The same can be said for the aspiring basketball player that is only 5′ 9″ tall. He or she may be a *basketball player* however, a 7′ 4″ player will alway have the advantage.

I believe, as you are reading this book, you know what magic can do and you are seeking to advance your knowledge and proficiency. That is fine if you know *what* you desire. Knowing how to achieve it is the only thing to question. Knowing the destination allows the individual to plot a course.

In the past, Satanists have been driven underground and persecuted. Pagans, Atheists and Satanists are differentiated because *most* true Satanists believe in Satan's existence and know what *Satanic Power* can really do. It is this factor that allows the proficient Satanist to practice Satanic Magic and achieve that which he or she truly desires. This is the essence and truth of Satanic Magic.

Whether a love potion, spell, curse, rite, invocation, or ritual, competent Satanists consistently hand-deliver the cognitive and magical *goods*. It is for this reason that we do not judge one another's magical attributes and abilities; we celebrate each other and recognize every person is an individual and not a sheep. When Satanists learn certain things about magic and can achieve certain new heights of magic ability, we celebrate those Satanists. It is for this reason, we remain together via an *unseen bond* which is Satanic Magic, performed in the name of Satan!

I am often asked how my belief differs from the *"mainstream"* Satanism of Anton Lavey. For the past 25+ years, I have worshipped Satan and His ruling council, *The Hosts of Hell*. Satan and demons exist in a curvilinear expanse; a dimensional offset from human physical reality. Sincere students of Satan (et al) can access the communication ingress with dedicated study and practice of Satanic Magic, Satanic Rituals and meditation techniques passed along in Satanic grimoires.

Inviting Satan and demons to your magical workings, in my experience, empowers the coven (or the sole practitioner) to accomplish those things believed to be beyond human grasp and in some cases, totally beyond human comprehension. I respect Anton LaVey and appreciate his contribution to the Occult as a whole *however*, he did not believe in **Satan**, which categorizes him as an *"atheist"*. He coined the term *Satanism* for his church however, there was no true *Satanic Power* involved.

As a staunch student of human nature, Anton realized in order to make his philosophy attractive to others, he would need to successfully combine elements of mystery, occult, secrecy, darkness, execrable evil and of course, entertainment.

Building upon his observations of human nature, he quickly characterized a *"persona"* of Satan that would aptly serve as the *'center piece'* for a humanistic theology of *"anything goes"*. Anton claimed Satan had kept the established church in business since the beginning of time so he set out to build an order of Atheistic doctrine powered by *"Satan"*. There was certainly a shock value involved.

Anton LaVey gave the world a guided tour of his new *Satanism* complete with celebrities, wild animals, rituals, scandals and sex. Opening the front door of the **Black House** at 6114 California Street in San Francisco was, for unwitting members of society, similar to landing on another planet. The media frenzy was akin to the *carnival-like* atmosphere of Anton's past. Anton wrote articles and newsletters that eventually became part of his book, *The Satanic Bible*. There was only one thing missing from the Satanic ignominy...........*"Satan"*.

While I have personally witnessed Anton's fledgling humanistic theology grow from his brainchild to a *"catch-all"* repository for every maladaptive behavior known to man, one element remains omitted, to the point of irreversible elusion; *"Satan is still omitted from his modern-day Church of Satan"*.

I could attempt to make a riveting point about semantics or the profound hypocrisy of performing rituals in Satan's name while denying His very existence however, it would be wasted breath and an argument in which I have no desire to participate. One thing Anton was correct about; *"Satanism simply means something different to each and every person"*.

In this book, I will delve deeper into a sampling of personal Satanic Magic processes; I shall write of that subject as Satan allows. You will need guidance to fully grasp parts of this book; especially when attempting to apply the concepts and practices for the very first time. You should not attempt this alone; for no matter your intelligence level or ability to correlate these postulates, science and reason are but a small part of Satanic Magic knowledge and magical proficiency. Remember, at one time in human history, very intelligent individuals stood tall and proclaimed *"The earth is flat"*. Preconceived notions can be quite costly and equally embarrassing.

If you are serious about learning the truth and magnitude of magic, I strongly recommend performing the *Ritual of the Black Flame* (found in my *Book of Satanic Magic*) before proceeding with practical applications; this is also true for the entire set of the *Sanctum of Shadows* volumes. During this ritual, ask *Satan, Lucifer, Samael, Azazel, Leviathan* and your *"Demonic Familiar"* to open your mind to accept that which may seem unreasonable or even impossible. Satan knows these words that I write because *He* has given them to me to share with you. He has been called the *"Father of Lies"* however, for more than twenty-five years, He has only revealed indisputable truth to me; *His* servant.

I will now ask you to set aside your preconceived ideas and notions concerning magic and Satanism. Just as a child must experience things in order to learn, so shall you experience that which may *burn your hand* in order to fathom particular principles. The number of times you metaphorically *touch the stove* is totally up to you.

Our physical world is a framework that serves as our "symbolic prison cell". Some incarcerations are longer than others and some lucky few are given an opportunity to see the world just beyond the *bars and walls* of this physical world. I have seen that which is just on the other side and as His devoted *scribe*, I will share with you as He directs.

For the reader of this work, I believe one of *"four possible points"* will be his / her conclusion: **1)** babbling for the unbeliever; **2)** glimpses of shadows for the dabbler; **3)** a form in the void without comprehension for the sincere beginner and **4)** a Satanic *Valhalla* and unearthing for the true, dedicated and studious follower of Satan.

The entire collection of these Satanic volumes were written for the *Searcher* however, *this* volume has been written for the true, sincere Satanist.

Many of the precepts will make little or no sense without a solid foundation in the Satanic. While those individuals of other beliefs may receive some value from its use *in general terms*, only the dedicated student of Satanism will fully grasp and appreciate the subtle messages incorporated herein.

Satanists of certain cognitive and magical abilities and capabilities will find each piece of this puzzle fitting snuggly, yet unforced, into place. For those kindred spirits, I dedicate each and every word, syllable, letter and sign upon every sentence herein, under the entire canopy of the nighttime sky.

Satan and your *Demonic Familiar* must play a vital role as you attempt to put this information into practical application. With their assistance, you will be empowered with the ability to unlock the secrets of the unknown. I have written this work to be embraced and easily understood without over complication.

Now, approach your Satanic altar with an open mind, outreached hands and submit to the *Will* of our Father, Satan. May you succeed in becoming a proficient Satanic practitioner. *"Cum Amico!"*

This book is dedicated to Satan, members of my "Patriarchal Coven" in Germany and my home coven, Magnum Opus.

Satanism

"Peace will never exist without compromise."

Aleister Nacht

The world is overrun by injustice; such as the xtians persecuting Satanists. It does not matter to Satan if you call yourself a practitioner of the dark arts. No one will come to your aid from the xtian church however, we are given a solemn charge from Satan, the giver of truth, and we must move forward to advance Satanism. Through anyway or form we possibly can, it is for this charge and this divinity that I continue to share my thoughts with the world. It is my purpose to agitate the so-called *"living saints of the deceiving order"*. This I will do until my last breath and beyond.

I continue to speak against such factions as the hypocritical xtians. I do not hate xtians; to hate would only destroying me (as a person) from the inside; no, I recognize that xtians are delusional people who have accepted an alternate reality - nothing more or nothing less.

While they believe their savior is going to come and receive them, I also believe one day it will be the downfall of those xtians; believing such nonsense! There are only a few documented claims in the history of the Catholic Church of any supernatural happenings. It simply does not happen so the xtian church is based upon a lie; plain and simple. Without this lie, the xtian church would cease to exist; if the truth were known, the xtian church would go out of business tomorrow. Now is the time that support of all such nonsense should cease however, since so many people blindly follow the xtian doctrine, I do not see that happening anytime soon. It is for this reason, I believe the xtians will continue to persecute anyone of any other belief.

There are only a few items in the Satanic toolbox that truly can be used against the xtians. It is not willpower; it is cognitive knowledge, Satanic Power and magical ability. We will delve into all three of these things in this book. I am not afraid to share this information with you; for I believe you, the reader, know the power magic holds.

I also firmly believe the xtian church and those associated with the church will, throughout time and forevermore until the end of such times, attempt to hurt Satanists and others of the left-hand path. They have spilt more blood of the Occult Arts than any other organization in recorded history. Satan realizes that while humans have a choice, sometimes their choices are limited by their surroundings. It does not really matter to Satan however, He expects His children to stand tall and strong in the face of adversity.

For that reason, xtians blame Satanists for murders and torture of innocent children. It is not with out reservation that I make the blanket statement that a church itself is not evil; it is however, human membership that forms the organization. The organization is evil and I do believe that one day the organism within the organization, will be the downfall of society if corrective actions are not soon taken.

However, we all believe in our minds that certain things are good and certain things are bad. This has been indoctrinated into us from a very young age. As a matter of fact, from the time we are born, we are molded to live in this world under certain regimes and paradigms.

One such regime is the xtian church which has worked diligently to hurt people who have only tried to communicate truth. For that reason, they have been maimed and/or murdered.

Over time, we develop many defense mechanisms and one of those mechanisms is against "so-called" evil. It allows us to justify certain actions to ourselves when in fact, these actions are nothing more than our parents' beliefs by proxy. The idea that we would do anything that would be totally against our own belief and / or rational ability is absurd.

Evil is an *acquired taste*. We are taught from the time that we are very young that god is the only good thing in this world however we learn over time and over years of practice that not everything called *evil* is necessarily *bad*. As a matter of fact, many things that are called evil by the world's standard are not bad at all. Some of those things are *very good* for our human development.

From the time that we are born, we actually have a hole in the middle of our aura. As we grow, we spend a lot of time trying to fill that hole and over the years, we find ways to redirect certain feelings from that hole.

From Satanism, I have learned this energy, and the feelings that are associated with this energy, is not simple to understand or control. It certainly is not something that comes naturally for everyone however, it is something that can be developed over time. As with evil, this ability is an acquired taste which most people, even the ones who have mastered it, cannot easily define or explain (*je ne sais quoi*).

Have you ever been really lost, driving around for hours, not knowing where you are? Have you wanted to find a place to pullover, stop and look at a map? Before the days of the global positioning system (GPS), the driver would have to stop and ask someone *"Where the hell am I?"*. In my opinion, Satanism was a lot like that years ago. If you were a Satanist, you did not stop; you were always in a *"bad neighborhood"*, figuratively speaking. If you knew where you wanted to go, you could never really get there because there were always others trying to block your way. Being a Satanist was always dangerous; very dangerous. Do not believe the xtian church has ever been concerned with harmony, love and acceptance.

I can remember the 1980s and the great *"Satanic Panic"* scare. Everyone was afraid of Satanists. You would never reveal you were a Satanist to anyone for fear that you might be physically attacked. It was quite honestly a modern day *witch-hunt* so it really did not matter what your thoughts were, what your beliefs were or your ideology / theology. If you were branded a Satanist, you were *"evil and bad"* and according to the xtian church, that belief has not really changed that much over time. In today's popular culture, being a Satanist is more acceptable and you're not really seen as the *Devil Incarnate*. It is now a wonderful time to be open and honest about everything..........or so it would seem. Just like racism, religious hatred and persecution remains *"alive and well"*. In a world of technology and informational enlightenment, society still holds on to the stupidity and prejudices of the past. Unfortunately, it seems to be *deeply embedded* in the human DNA.

I remember very clearly what I felt the first time that I read the *Satanic Bible*. It was almost as if I had found '*a true home*' and I felt like I really connected with Anton LaVey. I believed what he had written and it seemed as if he was *speaking directly to me* and no one else. I still feel that way when I read certain sections of his books however, I discovered over time, being a Satanist was more challenging than just buying a book.

The fact that his books explained a little about magic and ritual was amazing to me however, the fact of the matter is, it did very little to explain how to practice Satanic Magic or the philosophy. It was not until I joined a coven that I truly understood that there is another side of magic; not just a theme and *certainly not* simply a buzzword contained in literature - for the first time it meant something real and tangible.

On a primitive level, the word "*magic*" holds power for many Satanists. I will say that, over the years, I have found there are certain ways to expand one's magical knowledge.

If a person diligently practices magic, he/she may become quite proficient however, if a person believes he/she will become proficient by reading a book and not learning the material or experimenting to find their desired magical pathway, he/she will ultimately lose interest and drift to the next trend or fad. These lost souls are doomed to repeat this cycle until accepting the fact that magic requires investment and without the investment, they will always be *"on the outside looking in"*.

Demoniac

"Satanism is not a religion although some claim it is. I have never claimed Satanism is a religion."

Aleister Nacht

Satanism may have certain established dogmas and rituals however, it is not (in my opinion) a religion. This is very important for the Satanist to realize because a religion requires certain *conformity to ideas and / or dogmas*. Satanism does not. If you find that you are ever involved in a *"religion situation"* so to speak, you should begin to question everything involved. Satanism does not mandate required dogmas nor any required steps. This is important because for the Satanist, he/she must remain open-minded as I have previously emphasized.

You must remain open-minded and you must accept some things that are going to be foreign. You may even chuckle when you read some of these things however, rest assured, these things are real. You cannot see the *wind* however, the wind is real and you certainly can see the effects of the wind although you may not see it blowing. Electricity is invisible while you can see sparks and you can see electricity *arching* however, it can kill you; there is no doubt, it will kill if you are unprotected.

Magic is the same way. You may see the fluid movement of magic although you may never see magic itself; as elusive as the wind, magic will cause your wants and needs to become reality. Just because you cannot see it, does not mean that it is not there.

We use only a very small part of the brain and that is the key to understanding magic. For Satanic Magic, we utilize an additional part of the brain, not only for knowledge, but to harness the telepathic power of magic.

The fact that you are holding this book in your hands allows you to take advantage of the knowledge and practices I had to learn the hard way; mostly through *trial and error*. You will not need to "relearn" those lessons however, if you do not heed my warning, you may very well end up in the same place as the person ignoring the proper precautions around electricity.

Rituals are, in my opinion, the ultimate *"dance of death"* if not performed correctly. During a ritual, you are taking energy and forming it to your __Will__. Just like forging a bullet to be used in a gun, magic is similar during rituals. You will bring certain *Beings* into performances with energy; this is very dangerous as some demons will not play *nicely*. Demons are not "pets" and you should take precautions because you may not be able to during the ritual work.

As a whole, ritual is therapeutic and performing a ritual should give you a nice return on your investment; not only because of the magical working but it should make you feel closer to Satan and / or your respective *Demonic Familiar*.

If you do not feel closer, you obviously are not doing the ritual the correct way. Ritual work (in itself) is an art form. I've been very fortunate to observe many great masters of Satanic Magic perform their individual rituals and I can say they all have one thing in common; they are master Satanic Magicians and are always in tune with the spirit-filled demonic world as well as Satan Himself.

During any magical operation, you will call upon certain demons to perform work for you; whether delivering a message or delivering a death sentence through hate. Calling upon such demons can be dangerous. If you dance with the Devil, your day may come very soon to pay. The demons themselves will help and they often enjoy the manipulation, as performed by a skilled magician.

I know many demons and I have my favorite demons who I call upon. I have my "familiar demons" that assist during ritual work however, some demons can hurt you, even to the point of fatal results. Those events, we never "hear about" since their story is taken to the grave with the practitioner.

These demons are out for themselves and their personal gain. They are the demons who live in the outer limits of the Satanic. Satan Himself, has banished some demons to remain outside of the Inner Sanctum simply because they are more concerned with hierarchy and anarchy. There is no place in Satan's Court for those who are only out for one thing; themselves!

Without any giving whatsoever and without observing any of nature's laws, they *"take and take and take"* without replenishing. They are like bottomless pits; a vacuum that creates an empty space that will never be filled. These demons are more than anxious to appear for a uneducated "dabbler" and soon, the unwitting fool becomes the slave through relentless demonic curses and abuse. As stressed before, demons are not pets. They are very intelligent, motivated and skilled; they enjoy tormenting those willing to open the portal.

True Satanists are not like that and while I agree Satanists usually place themselves first among humans in the physical realm, there must also be respect given to the one we worship.

One example is the highest of Satanic holidays, which is the Satanist's birthday however, to ignore all the laws of nature is not Satanic - it is anarchy; it is chaos and there is no place for those things in true Satanism.

I do believe there are Satanists who truly do practice rituals without knowing what Satanism is; it is almost akin to the atheist who claims he or she is a Satanist. That could not be further from the truth. Sometime in past history, these terms have been used interchangeably however to the true Satanist, the worshiper of Satan, Demons and Devils, it simply is not true.

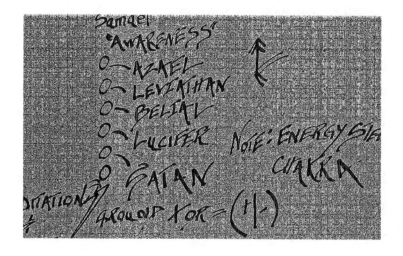

Ascendancy

"There is a common denominator; a secret that people overlook trying to find "something". Our dimensional reality is governed by a "quid pro quo" verisimilitude, tangibility and truth.......an unchangeable, undeniable, natural law. If a seed is not planted in the earth, the <u>Planter</u> should not expect a harvest. To expect "something for nothing" is stupidity. To Give = To Receive"

Aleister Nacht

The fact that atheists believe in nothing reaffirms the fact that they do believe in something. Satan is the king of this world and even the xtian bible admits this fact. Selling a product requires a "sales pitch". It doesn't really matter what someone wants out of life, Satanism is a *"last ditch"* effort for desperate people; *"It's as simple as selling your soul........."* Many times I have witnessed a conversation as such; *"I want to sell my soul so I can have money."*

So, if the soul is really worth anything at all, instead of selling it, why not use it? Quite honestly, it doesn't matter if you want to sell your soul; no one really cares about your soul, more especially "**_Satan doesn't care about your soul_**".

Through fables, folklore and xtian tales, the uneducated seem to believe Satan (or any other being) would want to actually buy a person's soul. I know people will pretty much do anything for money; that is simply a fact of life. Believe it or not (in our reality) everyone has a price and you can buy anyone if you meet their price during their time of need. Satanism, on the other hand, is not about your soul. Satanism is more about your natural abilities and how to integrate those abilities into the world of Satanism.

If you have a natural ability to be a "mover and shaker", being a Satanist will certainly help you in that endeavor. Being a Satanist is more than just knowing how to achieve something, it is about going and getting that which is desired.

This means working hard and taking what you want from someone not using it or the person asks you to take it from them. Saying this (in itself) teaches that you, as an individual, are the most important of all people on the face of this dirt ball, we call earth and because of that, you are the ultimate god. You are the king of your own destiny and you can make things happen however, you must work for them. Satanism is not about shortcuts; you are not going to be able to dedicate yourself to Satan and find that the world around you is any easier to negotiate. The topography of the landscape, whether it is corporate, cultural or societal, will not bring fortune and fame unless you are so inclined to go and get it! That is not what Satanism is and Satanism will not reward you for doing *nothing* in fact, I do not know of anything (or any purpose) that will reward you for doing *nothing* to help yourself.

This is nature, as in the animal kingdom, every species must work to survive. Anton LaVey summed things up very well when he said *"Satan represents man as just another animal, sometimes better, more often worse than those that walk on all-fours, who, because of his "divine spiritual and intellectual development," has become the most vicious animal of all!"*

This remains true today as the theology of Satanism is not about acquiring earthly goods; while earthly goods may be important to your overall endeavor, it is not the *ultimate power*. To wield *power* you must achieve *power* because you cannot delegate that which you do not have. In order to achieve *power* you must go and get *power* , which is usually accumulated *little by little* over time.

Power, just like money, is either given to you through birth right (i.e. inheritance) or you earn it on your own (i.e. the self-made millionaire). If you earn and accumulate wealth and power on your own, you will develop a natural intestinal fortitude enabling you to handle those things that come your way; defending your acquired fortune. Those who constantly tell you how successful they have been are self-consciously insecure and are usually lying to over compensate for their stupidity, failure and primal need for attention or recognition to validate their incompetence. Their pathology usually extends to impotence and inability to successfully satisfy sexual partners.

I am often amused when I hear people say they are powerful; the powerful people are the ones who never admit they are powerful simply because they have no reason to brag and nothing to prove. They know they hold the power, whether it is knowledge, wisdom, money, assets or anything else of value that gives them their power and it doesn't matter what a person has that gives them their power (also called leverage). Leverage is the most simple law of the land.

You may be required to defend your power and you may have to physically defend your power, depending upon the circumstances. While this occurs less frequently in modern time, in the past, a kingdom had to be defended with blood. In our world today, we wield an ink pen in much the same way that, in years past, the sword was used. We use it to cut people into small pieces; we use it to end their career; end their life; end their freedom and, as a person, make them disappear forever.

Leverage is most important in a game of pawns. Leverage can emulate power; it is an intangible substance that will give you power over those who may have money; it will influence positions and allow a person to move their chess pieces on the board without the other person resisting.

It is what allows a person to be able to take what they want from the other person without a fight; it is that cold steel against the throat that allows a person to take another person's freedom; it is a very powerful intangible and leverage makes our world function. We witness it everyday in the newspapers, on television, on the radio; those able to do things to each other without resistance because of the leverage.

Leverage may equate to money and leverage can be used with magical power. The way that a person uses that leverage says a lot about them. as a I am not referring to laurels; there is nothing moral about being a Satanist and I do not care about a person's morals or what they say right or wrong may be in their opinion. What is important is reality and the leverage that I hold over a person, applied at just the right moment can make that person do what I want them to do. Satanism does not teach any certain morality; we all know that one day we die; that is a fact of nature. Our story however, does not end there.

Inexorable

"Definition of Good and Evil: Good is what you like. Evil is what you don't like."

Anton LaVey

No one lives in this *physical* world forever. The fact is, no one has ever lived over 150 years in the physical world. Many people ask what happens when you die and we will discuss that later however, what I want to focus on right now is the definitive fact that Satanists must do, *are obligated to do,* our very best to improve our abilities while we are able. There is a reason why a wounded or sick animal goes away to die alone. The knowledge that they are sick and unable to defend themselves or remain within the social hierarchy is the very reason. In some Satanic covens, this natural occurrence, while delayed as long as possible, also transpires this way.

Society is the same way and humans play a game of power. When reaching a point when he/she no longer has power, they will either leave the power base or will continue to compete until being consumed by the very power they are trying to retain. One thing remains true, with power, authority and leverage, a person can construct a comfortable life, if desired.

I have never understood those individuals who fight such a great battle only to lose their nerve when it comes to finishing a fight. Having your enemy's jugular vein exposed is part of the battle and to me, this is to be savored and enjoyed before the actual kill. It is ultimately the best part of the battle, in my opinion. Some people may lose their nerve and believe that in showing mercy, they will be *shown* mercy. That is simply not true!! By showing mercy, you reveal that you are weak and weakness is not mercy. The two are very different. Mercy wastes time and time is always in limited supply.

Showing mercy to someone is something that you can do and you can feel good about doing however, showing mercy during battle is just stupid.

When an opponent reaches the point of surrender, showing mercy may be appropriate at that time. If a person is still fighting however, there is no reason to show the mercy; for if they can take your weapon from your hand, they will certainly place it deep into your chest. Keep that in mind...........always.

To have pity upon someone is different than mercy and it is certainly different from anything you will see during a battle. A person will not pick a fight (or should not pick a fight) if they are not prepared to deliver the final blow and decide the matter quickly. Battle is not for the "chicken hearted" and any conflict will certainly bring to light the very worst of human nature. May history always be our teacher, mentor and advisor.

The human can be a brutal animal and will actually start a conflict so he / she can destroy the other person. In my humble opinion, this is one of the best tactics when it comes to strategy however, only use this tactic when you know you are able to end the matter to your satisfaction.

If you pick a fight, the opponent may kill you (metaphorically speaking) so you should be prepared to kill the opponent (*metaphorically* speaking of course). The survival catalyst prevails and in Satanism, it is the most important drive. Choose your battles wisely and decide the matter with the final stroke or swing of your symbolic sword. To do so, will ensure your victory.

War itself, is a human entanglement. There are no other animals on the face of the earth that can plan and execute a complex strategy; possessing the power to totally annihilate the other. Humans can wage war and often do. There two things that can always turn a warrior into a ignoramus; underestimating the opponent and unjustified mercy. By the same token, mercy often manifests through the execution of a person (*metaphorically*).

Whether *executing* an employee by terminating their employment or executing them in the literal sense on a real battlefield, to show mercy, you must be willing to accept your own defeat.

Let me reiterate, if you show mercy and your mercy has not been fully reckoned, you run the risk of being destroyed. Certain matters are decided in the blink of an eye and the fate of the person can be decided in a whisper. So many times throughout history, an entire population or segment of society has been annihilated simply because they were ill prepared for war.

Have you ever noticed how people are drawn to sports superstars? Do you know why? It is because *deep within our psyche*, humans long for the power, entertainment and sportsmanship as the Romans did within the walls of their coliseums. We want to see the gladiators come out swinging their large swords. We want them to beat each other to a bloody pulp, until the weaker of the two, is dead! Our society, so some people want to believe, has evolved to the point where those thoughts do not occur anymore and will not occur anymore yet, that is not true. It happens every day and the point is, we do not look at the situations as life or death; we view it as sports, competition and entertainment.

We also cheer and applaud for our heroes. Humans must have heroes and leaders. Some leaders are good; some leaders are bad; some leaders will lead an entire population to success while others will lead an entire country into destruction, death and the possible elimination of that segment of the population from the face of the earth.

Before World War II, Adolf Hitler rose to become dictator of Germany through merciless displays of Nazi power. People are naturally drawn to power and powerful individuals. Hitler came very close to annihilating not only the Jews, but other demographic groups as well. The truth is, Adolf Hitler persecuted anyone who did not fully support *Adolph Hitler*. The Nazi party controlled everything and everyone in Germany. It was a *Nazi Party* desire for everyone to conform to the will of the organization and so, their persecution of the population was not just focused on the Jews (*or any other race or religion*). Homosexuals, the mentally ill, and any others deemed *"undesirable"* in their society also fell victim to the Nazis. Those groups were simply eliminated from the face of the earth.

World War II was a very dark time in human history (not only for Jews) and it clearly illustrates how brutal humans can be towards one another. For the most part, humans lookout for themselves and their interests. If you are not a member of the *group*, you may very well find yourself segregated and alone to fend for yourself.

I will not say that Satanists will look out for each other unequivocally - that would mean Satanists accept anyone into their midst and blindly protect one another, which is not true. I think it is fair to say that Satanists may accept other people but are not required to fight for those people. For example, if a person were in trouble, whether with the police or with other groups of people, a Satanist would not be expected to go to their rescue if they were not right in their dealings. If they *wronged* everyone and created enemies, no one from the Satanic coven would go to their rescue because their situation was "self-induced". Survival of the coven is always considered before entering a conflict.

Support, love, kindness and acceptance are human forces and it does not matter what organization you belong to or what club you belong to, if you wrong enough people, those people will in inevitably seek revenge. Satanism is no different. There is a lesson to be learned; *acceptance may be required for a Satanist to join a coven however, no one is required to endure being treated with a lack of respect or hostility for any reason.* Belonging to a Satanic coven does not mean your Satanic coven will fight every battle for you. If you are right, just and fair in your dealings with other people, you will be supported by other Satanists but the coven will not support a lunatic who has gotten into a bad situation through his / her stupidity, ego or actions.

Satan demands that you are accountable and without that principle, you are not conducting yourself as a Satanist. You must also demand accountability from those around you and you must not only expect, *but demand* equal treatment. Justice in itself, has nothing to do with morality. It does not matter what *organization* you belong to however, to do someone wrong, just simply because you want to do them wrong while expecting a Satanist to come and protect you............ that will simply not happen.

Finsteres Schloß

"It's too bad that stupidity isn't painful."

Anton LaVey

The Satanic Sanctum is a solemn and sacrosanct place for the Satanist; the room which is dedicated to their practice of Satanism. The Satanic Inner Sanctum is not only the room for performing magical rites and rituals, it is also a comforting, safe place to go for most Satanists. Many decorate the Inner Sanctum with whatever they feel is important to their coven or the individual and for their comfort, it is almost like being surrounded with your favorite things which brings a certain joy for the practitioner. In doing so, the magic power and positive energy are significantly increased.

While the feeling of being comfortable is important, in some cases, it may be *counterproductive* to become too comfortable. This feeling sometimes brings the practitioner to the edge of their magical performance. Those people who are comfortable or cozy will never seek other things; those people who are content with life will never strive for anything other than *status quo*. Ambition often comes from insecurity and a deep seated desire to master or achieve more than anyone. This is important and it results in new inventions; it is also the thing that causes new innovations. If a person is comfortable in their lifestyle, they may never seek to do anything else and ultimately, their life will pass them by.

Magic works the same way. Without a personal need; wanting or longing for something more or better, there will never be a true change. The person will continue to exist just like an animal in the field; no more, no less, no better, no worse.

You should never accept a magical operation which could be perfect, until it is *perfect*. I know some practitioners, myself included, have worked diligently over the years and continue to work diligently. I am not the most powerful Satanic Magic practitioner and I am not the weakest either. While my abilities may be better than some, they are not the best. You are reading this book and probably asking *"What could I do to improve upon my abilities?"* If that is in fact the question that you have asked, the answer may be obvious however, to improve, you must open your mind to other techniques that may be outside of your comfort zone.

For the ritual practitioner, knowing how to perform a ritual is important however, knowing how to perform a ritual and **make it your own** is ultimately more important. The ritual must "fit" you as an individual or it must fit your coven as a group. You should not be afraid to experiment with rituals because very few rituals must be performed verbatim. Let me say that again so there is no misunderstanding. The ritual must *"fit"* you as an individual or it must fit your coven as a group. You should not be afraid to experiment because very few rituals must be performed verbatim.

The ultimate satisfaction for the Satanist is taking a ritual, changing and molding it to produce exactly what is desired. As I have said before, not only are the results of the ritual important but the Satanic practitioner should receive emotional satisfaction from ritual performance as well. This is similar to having sex. What is the point of the sex act if there is no climax? You should enjoy the afterglow of your Satanic climax and you should take pride and pleasure from what you have accomplished during the ritual. In the case of a destruction ritual, you may not know the results for many, many days - perhaps even years. You can however, take comfort in knowing that you have performed the ritual, challenged yourself and the results are sure to bear fruit.

I have always felt comfortable in the darkness and enjoy the cool touch of fresh air outdoors late at night. I understand the attraction for our ancestors to open their souls and dance while praising the gods of the other worlds. I imagine witches around a fire concocting a potion for health (or perhaps other more *sinister* motives), asking for success and believing in their hearts and minds, their desires would be delivered. Satanism has been the instrument of "hope" throughout the ages and continues to be in our modern existence.

Magic will always fascinate the generations and there will always be those who are drawn to the secrets of the spirits. In my case, magic is in my daily life; whether writing about the subject, participating in rituals, reading and studying or meditating while increasing my energy, I find magic to be an endless source of questions and exploration of which I eagerly volunteer. My untiring pursuit of all things magic often leads me back to a common ground just as the circle around a pentagram perpetuates without end. It is a vast landscape that always holds a discovery just beyond the next hill. Magic and the operations of Satanism are also never-ending sources of amazement and discovery. I greatly enjoy witnessing others awaken the magician within and I share great pride in knowing I have taken part in their journey. Satanism is satisfying and fulfilling in an awe-inspiring fashion.

Satan reveals His magical secrets which you should quickly document in your grimoire for later reflection and contemplation. One of the most important elements of magical practice is the "building block" regiment that magical operations follow.

The grimoire allows the practitioner to record the nuances that may (or may not) be part of future successful rituals. After a ritual, I always take a few moments to write down what went right, what did not work, how the ritual progressed and the knowledge that Satan offered for your future workings. Continuous practice of magic allows the practitioner to receive Satanic blessings as residual energy cast during the working. I enjoy the hours following a ritual because I (and those with me) are renewed, regenerated and excited to discuss what just occurred. In the case of sex rituals, each member shares his / her perspectives.

I find the Satanic Sanctum to be a wonderful place to meditate. Sacrosanct residual energy remains within the sanctum for as long as a day after a ritual has been performed. This untapped reservoir of forces can be channeled during meditation and this allows for higher mental awareness and transcendence of astral planes by the practitioner. During Satanic meditation, taking the energy and converting it into usable and potent stimulus, opens the mind and spirit. Once you have experienced this immense power, you will be truly addicted and nothing else will fill the void or satisfy your magical longing.

Satanic Altars come in all sizes, shapes and compositions. Solitary practitioners will often have a small rectangular-shaped table filled with implements (bell, Athame, skull, grimoire stand, etc.) and trinkets they desire and hold sacred. The *Sigil of Baphomet* is usually displayed as a backdrop for the altar. Candles are used, not only for setting "*the right magical mood*", but also for lighting the room. Artificial lighting is not desirable during certain rituals. A chalice is used at certain times during rituals. I have been asked what *drink* is used by most Satanists and the answer is; "*Whatever you like*". The chalice is not required have to contain alcohol; in fact, I usually fill my chalice with tea when performing solitary workings. The substance is not important. Some altars are large and extravagant and during rituals, a woman lies on the ritual table and is referred to as the "Altar". **NOTE:** Our coven prefers a woman however, a man may also act as the Altar if desired.

Just as the tides of the oceans, magic ebbs and flows. There are certain times that magic contains more energy and taking advantage of those timely surges is beneficial for the Satanic practitioner.

The desires of the practitioner are carried directly to the source and his / her wishes are quickly granted by Satan and the Hosts of Hell. Those wondrous experiences open the door for more advanced magical operations. Transitioning from Satanic theory to magical application is always exciting for a new Satanist.

The lunar cycles do not control Satanists when planning rituals and magical workings. As I have said previously, more magical energy exists during a full moon and a new moon than at other times and this benefits by increasing the energy force available however, Satan nor Demons are bound by lunar cycles. They are free to manifest as they desire. When you invoke a demon through incantation, it does not matter what phase the moon is in at the time. If you are sincere in your intention and approach, you will get results; I have witnessed this countless times. The first manifestation resulting from a summons is also an exciting milestone for a new Satanist.

The calling of the guests from Hell should always be the first order of business when conducting a ritual or working. You must establish a connection early during the working so you can communicate your desires to your "guests". As the energy increases, the demon will connect with you while the ritual performed. When the events first unfold, some new practitioners may become frightened; this is perfectly natural, after all what he / she is witnessing for the very first time is in direct conflict with their personal reality. Even those who are excited about experiencing these manifestations will be taken aback when the event actually occurs. No amount of planning or mental preparation will be adequate to prevent the initial shock of the manifestation.

Anton LaVey wrote and spoke many times about Ritual Sacrifice by proxy. Satanists will perform these rituals from time to time to right a wrong done to them or their coven. Ancient Satanic cultures practiced *actual* sacrifice of animals and even humans.

In modern times, everyone likes to "smooth over" the sacrifice subject and use a "voodoo doll" analogy. In the past, destruction was not by proxy, teddy bear nor Barbie doll; it was a real sacrifice. This was no different from Islanders who threw a virgin into a volcano to appease a tribal god. The early Satanists believed blood (especially from a *newborn child*) held magical properties that would enable the energy to be heightened during rituals. Some covens believed that the infliction of sustained pain by the victim would greatly increase this energy thus, pain should be inflicted while the blood was taken from the victim.

For instance, increasing the pain of an animal (such as a goat) during a sacrifice would release adrenaline into the bloodstream so when the animal's throat was *finally* cut and the blood drained into the ceremonial chalice, increased power would be extracted by drinking the blood mixed with certain natural drugs.

Aleister Crowley experimented with the sacrifice hypothesis extensively while he lived in Sicily (at his *Abbey of Thelema*). One approach was to begin sexual intercourse with the animal and cut the animal's throat at the time of human orgasm. The blood was ingested and the higher spiritual plane (higher magical plane) was reportedly achieved.Crowley documented his impressions and magical results for future generations to use.

The workings of the ancients and magical pioneers such as Crowley, have taught us a lot in the form of "what works and what does not work". As Satanists explore the realm of magic in the future, I am confident other workings will be devised and new ways to harness and utilize Satanic energy will be discovered and cultivated. Until then, we must always reach for the outer limits of magical operation and strive to discover new territory for the generations of Satanists to come. We are responsible to pass our knowledge down to the coming practitioners who will learn basic and advanced (for our time) techniques of which they will use to fulfill their responsibilities to later generations. It is "we" who keep Satanism alive and well for the coming *Children of Satan*.

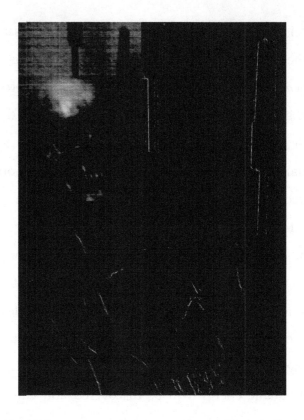

Sympathetic Magic

"Magic is believing in yourself, if you can do that, you can make anything happen."

Johann Wolfgang von Goethe

Over the years, *Witchcraft* has been closely related to Satanism. While both include the practice of magic, witchcraft takes a somewhat 'good *versus* bad' approach. Witchcraft claims to use dark or black magic and light or white magic to achieve the desires of the witch. Anton LaVey separated these two areas of magic in the *Satanic Bible.*

"White magic is supposedly utilized only for good or unselfish purposes, and black magic, we are told, is used only for selfish or "evil" reasons. Satanism draws no such dividing line. Magic is magic, be it used to help or hinder. The Satanist, being the magician, should have the ability to decide what is just, and then apply the powers of magic to attain his goals. Nature, in her ineffable wisdom, wastes nothing. Seemingly useless but parasitic or destructive persons should be used like clay pigeons: for target practice."

Anton LaVey

The origin of black magic can be traced back through history and actually has taken on many, many different façades. I grew up in southern Louisiana and was very much associated with and aware of *Black Magic* and *Witchcraft*. Another art I became very familiar with was *Hoodoo*. You may know what *Voodoo* is but did you know that *Voodoo* and *Hoodoo* are two totally different methods of magic?

Voodoo and Hoodoo originated in the African highlands and they are, by some analyses, almost polar opposites. Hoodoo has its own wonderful magical practice and I remember spending a lot of time in southern New Orleans at many of the teachers' homes and ritual parlors.

I learned many things from those *__wonderful women__* who shared so much of their valuable magical knowledge with me; a white boy. These ladies took me into their group and over time, became the family I longed for and never had.

They were very competent in their art; subtle yet focused, reserved yet extreme. They were very patient with me as I learned the subtle mechanics of their rituals. Magic was simply part of their daily lives and it was refreshing to discuss magic with them until the small hours of the early morning. **NOTE:** The skinheads who embrace hatred and violence while calling themselves *"Satanists"* will never experience true joy that brings people of all colors and backgrounds together to practice magic!

Hoodoo was more powerful and more impressive to me at a young impressionable age than any other magic I had previously been exposed to. My first Hoodoo ritual I attended was in the New Orleans French Quarter, two streets from the *St. Louis Cathedral (Basilica).* I learned some of the methods I use in Satanism today. I was initiated into the world of Hoodoo on a wonderful night, the full moon high in the clear sky, a stone's throw from *Cafe Du Monde.*

What always amazed me about Hoodoo (and inspired me to replicate) was how friendly and jovial the ladies and men who practiced Hoodoo were during the day however, at night and during the rituals, these people could easily cut your throat if someone crossed them. It was always something interesting to me; the fact that they took magic in stride and did what they wanted to do. It opened a world for me that made sense and it set the groundwork for the exposure to Satanism that would come shortly thereafter and change my life forever.

The magic rituals, candles, the darkness, the wonderful smells of food, the taste of wine and liquor, the wonderful sound of singing and chanting; all these things overwhelmed my senses and made such an impact on me at that time in my life. I don't know what would have happened to me had I not experienced that which opened the door and paved the way for my Satanic journey.

I believe the way those people treated me is ultimately what made Satanism so inviting. They were wonderful people and I could relate with them; I could feel what they felt and I knew being with them made me feel special.

I had never felt that way in all the years prior. They invited me into their domain and treated me as their equal. Clearly, I had little knowledge of the magical arts but they did not hold that against me. They did not make fun of me because I did not have the experience level they did; they did not mock me when I tried to duplicate their efforts and they had plenty of opportunities and did not. For this reason, I will always have a special place in my heart for those wonderful people who showed the way many, many times.

Sometimes, all we really need is someone to help guide us along the way and looking back over my life, I can identify those people who were chief influences at very pivotal points in time. My life has been good and bad; exciting and boring; wonderful and pure hell concurrently.

Some practitioners who have strong psychic abilities also have very, very strong sexual magic and in their practice of sex magic, they are able to do truly amazing things. It is a fact that sex and orgasm are some of the strongest emotional poles and strongest energy flows of a human being.

This means the practitioner who harnesses the energy from the sex act can literally move objects. Telekinesis is nothing new; it is been around for years and the proficient practitioner of Satanism may be blessed with the ability to move objects without actually having to do anything.

There is no connection directly between Satanism and telekinesis however, I will say the Satanist with the ability to control and move things with his or her mind is a powerful, powerful practitioner. His/her magic is second to none; an ability most are simply born with which is truly a gift. If they work diligently to hone their energy and sharpen their weapons, they become a force to be reckoned with.

For most people in the realm of Satanism, there are some undisputed facts for the magician. One fact is the true ability to improve upon that which must be improved; the second fact, to improve upon your technique, is imperative. It is very important and cannot be overstated. If you do not strive for perfection, you will never challenge yourself to improve to where you are totally proficient.

There are always those who are stronger, faster, can control more, are immune to others' powers and so forth. You must enter magical study and practice with the philosophy of continuous improvement. Some practitioners challenge themselves to become better and improve upon that which they do not think can be improved however, by doing so, far exceed other practitioners who accept or embrace *status quo*. Challenge the status quo and you will sharpen your magical abilities to a fine, point.

The same holds true for the beginning practitioner. He or she will be able to feel some changes before they actually happen but this has nothing to do with telling the future. This does not require psychic abilities; it requires alertness and attention. The beginning practitioner may be so in touch with his or her body and the external forces, he / she may feel the changes of energy just like feeling a rise or fall of barometric pressure. Remember, magic is energy and as such, it can be felt by those who remain astute.

A practitioner will only be able to do this after education, practice and a sincere desire to master the Satanic arts. Psychic abilities are not Satanic however, many people have psychic abilities although some do not have a true mastery of foretelling the future. Some shysters, cons or crooks may know a small amount about magic and foretelling of the future however, they are "readers of human nature" instead of magicians; more a student of human nature than magical arts.

Anton LaVey stated there are many people who can read other people and therefore tell them what they want to hear. These people can talk a person out of their wallet, purse, car, home, virginity, etc. This has nothing to do with magic nor does it have anything to do with psychic abilities.

Throughout my life, I have known many Satanists who have developed psychic abilities. Those who I have known to be authentic, are actually practicing Satanic arts and using their gift of psychic ability to improve their practice of magic; delving ever deeper into not only the psyche but the magical side of Satanism. Some would confess that it is more magic than psychic however, I believe they both can exist concurrently.

I've mentioned on my blog, the young lady who was abused all of her life but she had a special gift; the "candle trick". She is able to light a candle, extinguish it and within just a second, relight the candle with only her mind. It is really an impressive display and it is not a trick; it is real. It is not a trick candle, not a magician's trick, not a slight of hand, it is real magic and real cognitive and psychic ability as well. I have a great deal of respect for her, and others like her, to have the natural talent and extraordinary ability to be able to command this power.

Psychopaths have the ability to blend into our society and there have been serial killers who have been able to provide the socially accepted answers to certain questions. They have had good looks, charisma, charm and the innate ability to portray themselves as "one of us".

History has revealed underlying clues as to what their motivation may be. Like the events of 9/11, society went back in time and looked at these so-called warning signs that were there to be discovered from the terrorists.

The fact that no one discovered these things or brought them to other people's attention just amplifies the truth. We neither know what is good nor bad until the outcome occurs. We cannot tell the future; no one can with 100% accuracy. We can however, formulate a person's reality to make it what we want them to see and thus changing their reality to fit our reality.

Satanists have an ability, once the Higher Magic processes have been developed, to sense vibrations produced by another practitioner. Rest assured, the other person can feel your magical abilities and workings. You will sometimes be bombarded by the energy around you however, part of Higher Magic development is learning how to process these feelings and senses; which comes from dedication, devotion and sincere study of the Satanic.

If anyone could foretell the future, why did no one come forward to reveal the terrorist plot against the United States? I believe there were people who knew about this but it was not through a psychic power or other magical operation; it was through mistakes that revealed or leaked the plan.

It was man-made and could have easily been taken apart by a single person. The warning signs were there however, this had never happened before in history and no one thought anything like this could happen. After all, you would have to be a terrorist to think like a terrorist. We found out after the fact that this is not necessarily true, but at the time, it would have been crazy to accuse someone of a plot to commit suicide by flying airplanes into buildings. Our world changed dramatically that day. Now we look at several different things and we look at certain behaviors. We say these behaviors could be a terrorist act however, I say 20 years ago, these behaviors would have meant nothing. We as humans, must experience things in order to learn, as I have stated earlier. We will only know what we have experienced; we will only learn what we have experienced because we can only draw upon our memories. Memories work into magic because we will only know "magically" what we have learned magically and what is recorded in the grimoire. The magical book will provide the recipe however, we must experience those things record in that book.

In order for our magical operations to result in our desires, we must experience those things and write those things down. We must practice and evaluate the results. If we do not follow this simple but important process, we will neither grow magically nor become proficient in our magical operations. If you only take one thing from this chapter, you must experience magic and you must write down what happened magically; you must also practice, practice, practice. If you forget any step in this process, you will not succeed in your magical operations.

I have used perhaps a clear cut example where right and wrong or what is "socially acceptable or socially unacceptable" is clearly defined however, in many magical operations, the separation of good and bad may not be as clear. Again, there are no differences between white magic and black magic; magic is magic and the user determines in what manner the magic will be used. It is totally up to the user to define the desired output of that magic.

Some would say a magical operation is good while others would say the magical operation is bad however, it is totally up to the user to determine how that magical operation will be used.

One last thought on magic. Magic has no intention or "will" of it's own; no more than water desires to drown someone, magic does not seek to do our harm nor does Magic seek to do good. Magic is used by the practitioner for what ever the practitioner desires. Magic is neutral and is neither positive nor negative although the energy that results from magic can be composed of positive or negative. We know that electricity cannot exist without positive and negative charges. Magic is the same way; it cannot exist without positive and negative energy. The two together create the flow of energy that is then used to create a desire. A desire is created to change a persons reality.

Spend time with your ritual, working the ritual and preparing for the ritual. Your desires will consistently be met. The result of the magic may be good or bad but it will *never* be black or white. This has been a misunderstanding throughout the ages and it is my intention to clear this up today in this book.

Magic is simply magic and it can be used for any purpose. It has been used for many good and bad things throughout the history of man and it will continue to be used for good and bad purposes for the rest of our recorded history.

Historians tell us that in the dark ages, magic was forced underground and all magic became "bad" or black magic. I disagree with that and I know even during the darkest of human history, there are those who try to do something positive for another person who deserves it.

In keeping with Anton LaVey's rules and lessons he left us in books such as the Satanic Bible and *The Compleat Witch*, he often tried to prove the goodness of a person and the goodness of people while demonstrating not everyone is good or has good intentions.

He exemplified this and expanded upon the point by just simply saying *"The Satanist should judge as to the motivation and the motives of another person. Do not let another person persuade you of yet another person's motives; the color of an animal cannot be hidden for eternity. An animal that has stripes will one day reveal those stripes."* A person is the same way. If it is a person's true nature to be evil and cruel, they will show that side of their personality one day and will not be able to hide it *forever*.

Die Rohe Unkontrollierte Magie

"I was not content to believe in a personal devil and serve him, in the ordinary sense of the word. I wanted to get hold of him personally and become his chief of staff."

Aleister Crowley

In a prolepsis of Satanism, there are only a couple tactics you can use in order to control energy. Harnessing energy is as difficult as harnessing a lightning bolt. It is essentially the same theory and your abilities must be such that you are proficient.

One way of developing your ability is to develop spatial orientation and spatial awareness. If you look around you all the time, remaining at a heightened alert level, you will be able to recognize some situations before they actually occur. Some people interpret this as being able to tell the future; they are two totally different things. The attentive practitioner, efficient in the Satanic arts, will be able to know when changes are soon to occur resulting in his/her desires being fulfilled.

This is different, and I must repeat, this is much different than using a demon as deliverer of your desire. This is also quite different than throwing spells because the practitioner can almost feel the change before it actually happens.

You have probably heard of someone injured early in life and because of that injury, they claim to be able to feel when the weather is about to change. This is true; they do feel the change however, it is not premonition nor is it the ability to foretell the weather. It is simply the changing barometric pressure which affects the person's joints, tendons, ligaments and ultimately their entire body.

Change is inevitable. "The more things change the more they remain the same" is very much true and Satanists embrace change. We know change is necessary for things to improve and for us to grow as individuals and ultimately, as Satanists. As practitioners of Satanic Magic, we know change is mandatory because without change, the magical operations will be useless. Controlled change is an important element for Satanists.

Spatial Orientation (to be aware of one's surroundings) is very important, whether it is in a crowded area with your hand on your wallet or whether you are walking down a dimly lit street at night, you must be aware of your surroundings and you must be aware of the things that can easily influence the elements around you. With magic, there are many, many influences; seen and unseen. It is important for the Satanic practitioner to know and be able to recognize these elements.

One of the elements is energy and as stated earlier in this book, energy is the force which causes life to be formed and it is also what causes life to burn out and die. Once all energy has been expended, nothing remains except an empty void. Being able to harness that energy and control it is one of the ultimate goals. When energy is controlled, a metaphorical "levee" can break; bringing great things including change.

Some Magicians actually practice certain rituals for nothing more than increasing their ability to create and harness energy. There may not be any other output to the process except being able to develop a strong energy flow and direct that energy flow. Such practice will certainly increase the practitioner's skill level.

So, what path is the correct path for the sake of this undertaking? Is it the path of least resistance that certainly sounds strange to someone who is not a Satanist? It is almost like saying you learned to love pain by having a root canal; quite the contrary. I found that by exploring the spiritual and the Satanic at the same time, I was actually learning about myself, as an individual.

You will be surprised how many people do not truly know who they are and that is not intended to be a joke. This is a discovery of the point, usually for the layperson who is new to this line of thought. Look at a situation through the eyes of the Satanist and learn what it is to be human.

I can't say those who have experienced this metamorphosis are truly satisfied or truly happy with themselves and it does not mean that you will know everything there is to know about yourself either. This is a journey after all. To become Satanic is to become human; to become human is the path of high resistance but greater rewards than a path of least resistance. This is always the way that the person can easily achieve whatever objective they strive for (because the difficult objective is the one truly worthy of achieving), is wasted on those who do not invest the effort or the energy to achieve.

For me, the decision was quite easy. Early on, I began to look at the alternatives in my life and this was probably the best thing that could've happened to me; not only in a literal sense but also a metaphysical sense. I found that delving into the world of the spirits was something exciting and enticing. It really peaked my interest, almost like a fish to water so to speak. I also found that by learning magic and learning about Satanism itself, I began to develop as a person. Personal development was a prerequisite for understanding and enlightenment.

If I asked you to honestly describe yourself, how would you begin? If you have been reared under a xtian theology, you would probably consider those values as part of your character. What you consider truth would depend greatly on your background since the past makes up our future and in some cases, it creates the future. If you embrace your past and accept that you are not a perfect creature, you will begin to realize what it is to be you. Acceptance will open the door to learning.

First and foremost, trying to be a perfect person usually contributes the most to the flaws in one's character; after all, you can be *too good for your own good* in my opinion. We are flawed to some way and in certain instances, this is what makes a human beautiful. When we recognize that we are not perfect, we realize true perfection. Perfection is not hypocrisy and lies. You cannot lie to yourself every day and achieve perfection. Just like parents who do not admit their children have problems, you can talk yourself into a fairytale far removed from reality. Accepting your imperfections is the best thing you can do for yourself and those around you.

If you view life from the xtian perspective, you will end up putting unneeded pressure on those you love; more than they can possibly withstand. Constantly being told they are *"not perfect and will never achieve such glory"* will honestly drive your family, loved ones and friends in sane.

Many times we see maladaptive behaviors that become maladaptive simply because they are suppressed to the point of denying humanity. To be human is to have certain wants, needs, requirements and lusts.

Without lust, the human species will not repopulate. It is natural, so why suppress the animal need? You are only lying to yourself when you say you can abstain from sex. If you look at a beautiful man or a beautiful woman, your animal instinct will take over.

I have witnessed those individuals who have placed so much pressure on themselves and on those around them, they ultimately cracked under the strain of lies. No one can live a lie forever; the truth will surface and often that truth can be much more ugly than if we would have just accepted that truth to begin with.

We are not perfect; we will never be perfect however, there is *One* that accepts us with all of our imperfections. Satan accepts us for what we are and He knows our limitations. He admits our achievements and our prospects, He also knows what we can do and what we cannot. There is no reason to lie or misrepresent the truth. For those who continue to lie to themselves, the truth will be a bitter pill to swallow.

There is a way to overcome; you cannot lie to yourself forever. The law of averages will catch up to you and usually, in those cases, the lie will be so huge at that point, it will bring much anguish and heartache when it rears it's ugly head.

Admit imperfection; embrace imperfection; continue to learn, grow and challenge yourself to attain better and constantly improve, knowing you have natural limitations. Without those limitations, we would not be human.

From one perspective to another, we try to understand what motivates a person, whether it is improving or whether it is lying - the objective remains the same. We as humans want to achieve more, do more and become more than sometimes physically or cognitively capable of achieving. This is really okay and acceptance is okay as well. There is no law, no dogma, no theology in Satanism that requires perfection. Do not lie to yourself. Strive for the best and recognize that you may not achieve perfection and always give Satan the glory and the praise for giving what you have fought so hard to achieve.

Verständlich

"Magic is a science. It is the only science which occupies itself, theoretically and practically, with the highest forces of nature, which are occult. It declares and proves that the universe, in its totality as in each of its smallest parts, is subject to certain fluid influences and that science can prove this, the day that it will, to be the basis of all psychic and physical phenomenon. To operate with these forces, according to the laws which regulate them, it is necessary, first of all, to concentrate them in a point or on a given surface. One can, then, guide and channel them at will."

Pascal Beverly Randolph

Some people over-value themselves and while it's okay to have faith in your abilities and *more than okay* to have a modicum of ego, it is not okay to over-value yourself. It doesn't really matter if you think you are worth $1 million, supply and demand as mentioned in this book, controls the price that everyone is worth.

Satanists view life a bit differently than any other belief or any other system. We enjoy life, we enjoy living life, we like to take chances however, we are not reckless in our endeavors. Embracing risk does not mean you must be a reckless person. Our nature as Satanists is simple; sometimes enjoying life means we will take risks. As with anything, whether it is skydiving or swimming with sharks, risk is sometimes what creates excitement.

Many who are not familiar with true Satanism, often mistake the Satanic arts with drugs and other maladaptive behaviors. Drug use, in my opinion, can be a tool used by Satanists for rituals and magical workings however, caution must be used. Just as any tool can be used to kill, drugs can either heighten the awareness or capture the person and imprisoned them. For many people, the heightened awareness that drugs bring is actually the only way of enriching Satanic ritual. I do not agree with this however, I do not condemn it either. The method a person chooses to operate ritual working is totally up to them and I will not pass judgment on those who use drugs or a person who does not use drugs to heighten their awareness. I will simply caution the user again; do not be trapped because drugs can and will enslave you.

The subject of blind faith usually comes up for a new Satanist. I will say blind faith, in any situation, is a losing situation. What I mean by this is you cannot believe 100% of what a person says and you should never rely on one person's point of view too many times. Cults have started and perpetuated through a philosophy of absolute dictatorship and I do not believe in nor do I advocate this type of behavior. If you wish to dedicate yourself to someone, you should weigh what you will be giving and what the return on your investment will be.

I believe many times cults are formed when one person sees they have absolute power over a certain group or demographic of the population. Without the absolute power, any person can question and be questioned, as in the aforementioned, the answer often is simply *"the way that it is supposed to be"*. As a Satanist, you should challenge authority (when appropriate) and ask "why am I doing _____, why am I following this person and what do I expect to gain and what is this person going to give me in return?" As I've said before, for a Satanist, questioning everything is always a necessity. To accept on blind faith without justification is not Satanic.

In the case of vengeance, Satanists are always drawn into the argument "Is vengeance really mine?" I say, in my opinion, the answer is yes, vengeance is always mine. There are however, some caveats. Depending on exactly what a person has done to a Satanist, sometimes other means of vengeance are necessitated. That is not to say a person that has wronged you by accident should be the point of abuse or other actions however, I will say that most new Satanist always ask the question.

I think it depends upon the specific situation and every situation is different; thus, should be judged accordingly. I do not believe "one-size-fits-all" when it comes to dealing with this situation for Satanic followers or Satanic worshipers. I will say that over the years, I have gained an experience level in vengeance and I believe it does not really justify vengeance in every situation; in fact, not only should you look at the individual situation but you should also consider the best course of action for you as a person. A Satanic practitioner does not have all the answers and simply because you have followed an initiation ritual does not mean you will have the answers for every situation. My best advice: look at each situation differently, evaluate and always, always use the option that is in your best interest every time.

There are those who think Satanism is just blindly hating. This is a misconception that is simply not true. Satanists are some of the most loving, compassionate, tender, caring and attentive people around. Just because we pray to a different god and shun established religion does not mean we do not enjoy sharing and being around other people. We have compassion; just as anyone else and we do not wish Hell upon anyone without proper justification. We have families, friends, loved ones and we know how to live, love, share and do it with a certain life balance. As a Satanist, we learn how to enjoy life and get as much out of life as we possibly can. It has been said "Any day on this side of the grass is a good day" and I totally agree with that statement; in fact, it is a very good philosophy to apply to your life. We should always seek opportunities that make us happy and add quality and value to our existence.

The subject of chaos (or chaos magic) often comes up in discussions with new Satanists. Chaos, by definition, means "a state of things in which chance is supreme; the inherent unpredictability in the behavior of a complex natural system (as the atmosphere, boiling water, or the beating heart); a state of utter confusion".

Satanism is not chaos and those who use the term Chaos Magic do not understand the principles of true magic. Those who say chaos is the secret to magic are simply misguided. It is not true! We are never *out of control* during a ritual or magical working and although the ritual itself may appear to be a bit frenzied and disorganized, it is far from that. Magic is always metered and controlled. Magic comes from good order while chaos is created using confusion and happenstance. The two cannot (and will not) exist simultaneously.

For the practitioner of Satanic Magic, one thing remains true; there is only an appearance of chaos (in some rituals) however there is no chaos (that is, out of control) when it comes to Satanism. The ritual is actually a well choreographed play or dance performance used to assemble elements into a certain chronological order for delivery of potent energy.

The ritual itself, begins and concludes with order and those partaking in the working should also be of good order. There is no reason to cause such a disruption resulting in a ritual not being closely guarded and controlled.

The term *magic* implies a control that delivers a potent and powerful direct energy. Many spontaneous actions in magic sometimes happen and certain events in magic may take place without the practitioner knowing exactly what the outcome will be. This is different from chaos and it is certainly different from confusion; not knowing the precise outcome of a ritual is different than not knowing if there will be an outcome. For the practitioner, especially the seasoned practitioner, magical rituals can (and often do) surprise and delight the practitioner.

Satanic Magic is an art form and being an art form means each practitioner or user will have different impressions on the use and the results. Some practitioners use what they call white magic (as previously discussed). I have often heard this term used in the art of Wicca. This art uses magic processes for doing good and not harming anyone. I agree, to some extent, in this philosophy however, just as Anton LaVey disagreed with the established definitions of white and black magic, I disagree with the idea that there is good and bad magic.

Magic inherently does not have a fitness, goodness or badness; magic is simply managing the flow of energy. I do not think of their magic as being good or bad and they may actually believe the results are good or bad, negative or positive, etc. Operations may differ and our interpretation of what we are doing may differ however, the magic itself does not change. Magic changes reality to fit one's motives and desires. If a practitioner performs a ritual for a desired effect, it is not black or white magic that results in his / her desires being met.

During a love spell for instance, the practitioner may say *"it is good (or white) magic"*; the person that is the object of this spell may say that it is bad. The reason why may differ however, magic can cause a person to like or love another individual for whom the user may not be worthy of such adoration or love. If a pedophile performed a magical operation, causing a child to love him or her in the same way he or she loves the child, this would be (by some people's standards) black magic.

Some practitioners would actually be appalled to hear that a pedophile performed a ritual or a spell to make a child want him or her in the same manner the child was desired. I would say in this situation, society determined that to be a pedophile and act upon this urge is socially unacceptable in this circumstance. This example would be black magic according to societal norms however, to the pedophile, this ritual or spell would simply be white magic. According to him or her, there would be no difference.

Kaltblütig

"To read a newspaper is to refrain from reading something worth while. The first discipline of education must therefore be to refuse resolutely to feed the mind with canned chatter."

Aleister Crowley

Magic results from a Satanic Magic process, and there are steps to be taken. If any of these steps, by chance or intention, is omitted or is not performed efficiently, effectively, or precisely the way they should be performed, the output of the magical process will not be the desired results.

In life, our everyday events occur the same way. If you change one event in your day, the remaining events might not happen or they may not be as you planned them to happen. This is important because by changing any task (step), you change the result of the over all event. It is really simple to see that the link in the chain can be broken and will result in adverse effects; these effects may or may not necessarily be dangerous effects which is not the point to this dissertation.

The point is, if you are not receiving what you desire from your magical workings, you need to examine the steps in the process to identify what needs to be changed in order to produce the effect or the desire.

Without changing anything, there is no difference and as I have said before, stupidity by definition, is doing something over and over again and expecting a different result. I say this to make my point because there are many practitioners of the Satanic Arts doing the same thing simply because it has become second nature or even become unconscious dogma or ceremony, as opposed to real and powerful Satanic Magic.

View your rituals from a "step to step or task to task" methodology. It is inevitable that by truly analyzing the steps of your ritual process, the process will reveal weakness, muda, contradictions and useless drivel. How many times have you prepared a dish while cooking and omitted adding an important ingredient from the recipe? Perhaps you did not want to go to the market and pick up that essential item. Perhaps you did not feel it would make a difference in the dish you were preparing so instead of going to the store and buying the proper ingredients, you chose to not use the ingredient or chose to substitute the ingredient with another.

If you have done this before (I have), you know that the end result did not taste anything like what you expected and because you did not follow the recipe, the dish turned out being terrible or inedible. I have to laugh at myself because when it comes to going to the grocery store, I am the world's worst procrastinator and chose to substitute another ingredient. It ruins the dish every time.

My expectation for how a dish should taste is dependent upon these other tasks and these other ingredients with which, there is no possible way to duplicate the recipe. Magic is very much the same way.

If you do not use exactly what you need to use as a practitioner, you will not experience the desired outcome. I am not saying that you cannot substitute certain things in magic and get close to (a resemblance) the desired outcome. It can happen and produce the desired results.

I encourage a person to try different things however, if you experiment, you will not consistently produce the results you are expecting. For the practitioner of Satanic Magic, it is important to keep a grimoire (and keep it up to date) and record all of your magical workings. One small element may be the key to consistently producing your desired results. Without it, you negate the ability to consistently produce a certain magical effect. If this magical effect is only one part or one element of an overall system (a ritual having many different parts to be performed at different times such as on three consecutive *Full Moon* nights) it could have catastrophic results. You must remember that advanced Satanic Magic is built upon certain magical operations; these "building blocks" can be assembled in any manner and the combinations are limitless. You must know the combination and measure in order for a certain element or task to deliver your desired results consistently. When you need a specific result, experimentation is unacceptable.

For some practitioners, their magic practice will never result in two of the same things because they never take the time to document their magic in their grimoire. It is one of the most powerful tools in the Satanists' arsenal. Without it, your practice will become energy zapping because when performing a ritual or operation and you will never know, with any consistency, what the outcome will be. This is almost the same as having a map, but not having any names, streets or any cities identified on the map. Without having something that you can identify, you will not know where you are or where you are going. The Satanic practitioner must not accept any less; to do so will be at your magical detriment. The grimoire is a powerful tool that must be consistently used and revised.

Beholder

"The ecclesiastical description of Hell is that of a horrible place of fire and torment; in Dante's Inferno, and in northern climes, it was thought to be an icy cold region, a giant refrigerator. Even with all their threats of eternal damnation and soul roasting, Xtian missionaries have run across some who were not so quick to swallow their drivel. Pleasure and pain, like beauty, are in the eye of the beholder. So, when missionaries ventured into Alaska and warned the Eskimos of the horrors of Hell and the blazing lake of fire awaiting transgressors, they eagerly asked: "How do we get there?"
Anton LaVey

In the 60s and 70s, so many people were in the dark about Satanism (metaphorically speaking) because there was not enough information out there for people to make informed decisions.

I have the utmost respect for Anton LaVey however, as I have stated in the past, I do not believe 100% of what Anton revealed as his *Satanic Theology*. There was simply not enough information in the social consciousness to be able to accurately analyze his assertions.

Mike Warnke had written a book, *The Satan Seller*, and I remember reading this book and thinking *"What an idiot! This guy does not know anything about the Satanic Arts, Satanic Magic and has no real knowledge of Satanism."* He had no idea what he was writing and that fact became painfully obvious some years later, when a magazine published a news article after performing an investigation of Warnke. They found that everything he had stated in his book was in fact lies. He had never been a Satanic High Priest or even a Satanist.

Mike had built quite a career and a ministry from selling the idea that he was previously a Satanic High Priest and in his book, he made allegations of Satanic activities that "his" Satanic coven was involved in; many of the different things were ultimately proven to be false.

I guess my point is to raise an awareness for the Satanist. People are selling things every day and people are buying things every day. Had someone performed due diligence, they would soon have found his entire timetable did not match up with *"his"* events (as others who knew him during the time in question attested) and the time that he claimed these events took place, could not possibly have happened. The entire situation was laughable and it represents the "Satanic Panic" decade that gave Satanism a *"bad name"*.

Over the years I have realized that no matter how much you try to caution a person about doing something that will harm them, it means nothing. The fact is, most people are going to "do what they want to do" and not think about the the catastrophic results. People learn by what they experience and that is why learning has to involve one of the five senses. We will never know more than we have experienced; whether it is through sight, feeling, etc. We must go through the actual experience and hopefully we will benefit from the event. Grab your grimoire and write, write, write!

While some people may take heed to a warning, others will simply choose to experiment or "test" a theory to determine if it is, in fact, an adverse effect. This can be good for the Satanist (such as discovering a new magical operation or new way to communicate with a demon) however, it often results in catastrophe. Set your limits and remain within the safety margins.

The Satanist must understand that which may or may not be an actual bad thing and choose to try something to determine the "goodness" (if it meets the needs, wants or desires). I am an advocate for trying anything new to determine if it is what you like; if you like the results you will probably consider doing the 'act' repeatedly. Some simply want to "see for themselves" and, of course, testing any hypothesis makes logical sense. After all, variety is the spice of life,

I have actually used testing extensively in the past while trying to learn what works and what does not work during magical operations.

My collection of grimoires documents the failures and successes of the decades of experimentation. The Alchemy of substitution, *less-versus-more*, temperature, timing, etc. is experimentation that frequently reveals hidden secrets for the Satanist. Can you claim an extensively documented grimoire worthy of interest or Satanic value? Start now and over the years, you will have a living testament to Satanic Magic.

It does not matter if one person may agrees or disagrees with the way that you perform a certain task, the methodology is totally up to you however, base your process upon that which you have witnessed and know to be true; in most cases, scientifically proven and documented in your grimoire. On my blog, I try to transmit information to my readers that may save some heartache, headache or other undesired results. At the end of the day however, it is truly up to the individual. Individualism is a Satanic characteristic. If there is enough objective evidence to prove something will harm you, why subject yourself? Do not take a needless chance.

A technique I use quite often is what I call *"Paraphrase Analysis"*. I rewrite something that has already been written so I can learn from others. These exercises are never published anywhere; they are only for me to work through and find those all important *"things unsaid or implied"*.

I first attempt to analyze the author's point and motivation. Asking *"Why has the author invested the time to write about this topic?"* is a great way to begin. This usually 'separates the vital few from the trivial many' (Vilfredo Pareto). Have you heard of the 80/20 rule?

Next, I view the word arrangement to understand the true meaning and why particular words were chosen by the author. For a writer, choosing the correct word is paramount; *"Words are tools that build ideas"*. **NOTE:** What appears to be misspelled gibberish to the general public, actually carries an important message for students of the occult. Spell check does not benefit the occult author.

In the past, before technology made communication fast and easy, Satanists would often communicate with other covens using benign articles or newspaper classified advertising. With only the need for "casual cover" from the majority of readers, messages could be sent without raising questions from the general public. This technique is still used in the technological world today. If you have noticed, it may actually be used in this book. Look and see!

After completing these steps, I begin to paraphrase the points the author has tried to make in the text. In communication, paraphrase is used by a Receiver to affirm understanding. It is not the only affirmation however, it is one that often reassures a Sender that the message has been received, decoded and fully understood.

When I have finished, I read the paraphrasing aloud several times. My brain begins to compare the original text with the paraphrasing and with a touch of Satanic understanding, the words take on a life of their own......*elaborately simple and simply elaborate!*

Chakras

In dedication to our Father and the Hosts of Hell!! Satanas vobiscum. Palas aron ozinomas Geheamel cla orlay Baske bano tudan donas Berec he pantaras tay. Amen . . . Evil from us deliver but . . . Temptation into not us lead and . . . Us against trespass who those forgive we as . . . Trespasses our us forgive and . . . Bread daily our day this us give. . . Heaven in is it as earth on . . . Done be will thy . . . Come kingdom thy . . . Name thy be hallowed . . . Heaven in art who . . . Father our. Eva, Ave Satanas! Vade Lilith, Deus maledictus est!! Gloria tibi! Domine Lucifere, per omnia saecula saeculorum. Rege Satanas! In the name of Satan, ruler of Earth, the King of the world, I command the forces of darkness to bestow their infernal power upon us and open wide the gates of Hell, And come forth from the abyss to bless this unholy treatise!

The subject of chakras often comes up and for many Satanists who truly do not understand the concept, the subject becomes a point of contention instead of knowledge of this (in my opinion, vital) subject matter.

Many Satanists 'duck out' when "touchy or feeling-related" topics are discussed at length however, the essence of Spiritualism, Satanism, Wicca, Witchcraft, Hoodoo and countless other occult belief systems practice magic using the chakras and certain exercises that develop the chakras and in turn, improve magical capabilities.

Magic aside, the chakras have been used throughout human history by those who understood the human as a "complex set of walking and talking systems". Realizing the holistic approach to health, magic and cognitive ability is critical for Satanists early in their journey. The development of the chakras is of prime importance.

The seven chakras are derived from Sanskrit meaning "wheels or disks of energy". Spiritual energy causes a transformation of consciousness and several physical changes in the body. When a chakra receives energy, it rotates and the sensation can be felt throughout the body. Meditation is not "mandatory" for Satanists however, use of meditation and the health of the chakras will certainly increase Satanic Powers beyond any expectations. Without this vital development and knowledge of chakras, the Satanist will not progress to Higher Magic processes, since the chakras will play a constitutive part.

While demons often deliver the Satanist's desires to the person and / or object of magical focus, it is the all-important connection between energy and magic that serves as a mandatory process step for successful magical operations including spells, curses, conjuration and invocations. It's the dormant energy that rests at the base of the spine waiting for the chakras to align in harmony.

Prana is the vital spark-of-life-force energy and without Prana, there is no life. Energy produced during controlled-breathing meditation travels through the seven chakras of the body. Problems with the seven chakras (individually or separately) will manifest in causing physical ailments of the body. If the chakras are free from obstructions and the path between each is well maintained, an awakening and flow of this vital energy begins.

During this process, the kundalini energy activates each of the seven chakras as they are ready. The movement starts at the Root Chakra, bringing awakening and higher levels of consciousness as it continues through the other chakras.

There are many reasons chakras may not be charged with energy or spin as necessary. Childhood traumas resulting from molestation or abuse, an overbearing or over controlling belief system, unforgiven emotional damage, denial, guilt, repression or a lack of attention may prevent a chakra from proper development or function. Soon afterward, everything is affected including posture, metabolism, breathing, heart rate and emotions. Diseases are often caused by repeated blocking of the pranic energy. These seven chakras store all your thoughts, deeds and actions you've committed in your lifetimes. The repression of emotions are the one's that cause pain, suffering, disease and death. Accepting your rejected feelings, feeling them deeply, finding something positive to love in them and forgiveness are the keys to healing your soul and disease.

Your beliefs result from repeated conditioning of the past and we all have them. If you had a strict religious upbringing, you were probably exposed to shame, overactive conscience and frequent feelings of imposed guilt. These repressed feelings are stored in your subconscious mind and are not easy to ignore; much less, delete from your mind.

Satanists are not immune from these feelings however, it is imperative that the Satanist recognizes and mitigates the issues these feelings cause. This is why the Black Mass, Satanic Pact, Selling the Soul or Satanic Ritual Initiation is very important for many Satanists - these symbolic actions represent cutting the cancerous feelings from the Satanist's body and mind while at the same time, severing ties with the past. Once the Satanist accepts and forgives themselves for being human, the healing can begin. This is the prerequisite that allows the Satanist to increase his / her magical abilities. You must eliminate all feelings of guilt, shame, self-pity, false obligation and the ability for anyone to coerce or control you through the manipulation of your feelings or emotions.

When first charged with an energy input, the chakras begin to vibrate. If energy input is constant or increasing, the chakra begins to spin and the RPM (revolutions per minute) increases, usually at a metered rate. The chakras rotate at different speeds determined by inputs, influences, internal and external factors.

The chakras are interdependent; occasionally linked together by energy and magic during successful magical operations such as spells, curses, conjuration and invocations. This is the area where we begin to separate the Students (serious practitioners) of the Dark Arts from those simply wanting to follow style, fashion and appear mystically educated.

Just as chakras can have a negative impact on your health, conversely, your health can have a negative impact on your chakras. The two are closely interrelated and a salubrious approach is a must for serious practitioners. A person must be dedicated to the principles of learning magic in order to become proficient. The association and connection between magical operations and the chakras is very relevant and important because without the health of the chakras, you will harm yourself much more while attempting magical rituals.

If you have ever been ill with the flu virus (influenza), you probably know that the entire illness is a process. It begins with perhaps a sore throat and runny nose as the virus takes hold.

You probably remember how bad you felt and how miserable the virus made you. It takes a while to recover from such an event and it really zaps your strength. Even weeks after your recovery, you may continue producing Phlegm (aka sputum, expectorated matter, mucous).......no fun at all. When your chakras are not healthy, you may not notice it immediately however, if you pay close attention to the signs, you will be able to take a preventive action instead of waiting to take a reactive approach after your immunities are unable to fend off the illness any longer.

The Root Chakra, the fused vestigial vertebrae (coccyx) located in the genital area, rotates the slowest of all chakras. Your survival, security, safety and primal erotic urges are grounded in this chakra.

All of the energies that reach the other chakras flow through the Root Chakra and so, if this chakra is unhealthy, you will not be a "whole" being. This is usually where the "root cause" of the magical impotence (and serious health problems) begins. Balance and moderation are very important for the health of any living creature on this earth.

Excessive smoking, drinking, drug use, overeating, high risk lifestyle choices, etc. will have a negative impact on your health. This has nothing to do with morals or any religious belief; it is a clinically proven fact.

The Root Chakra represents the most difficult chakra to repair maintain for many people. This chakra also comes with some personal "baggage" and letting go / putting the past permanently behind the person, while mandatory, can be a challenge and very, very painful. The Root Chakra is developed in the first few years of a person's life; up to the seventh or eighth year, dependent upon the person's rate of cognitive development. If the child is loved and nurtured by caring individuals, the rate and quality of the chakra's development will be healthy, resulting in an emotionally and physically well-grounded individual. The polar opposite of this precept is also true. Most serial killers have a history of mental and / or physical abuse during their childhoods which further reaffirms the prodigious impact resulting from such abuse.

Lack of confidence, suicidal thoughts / tendencies, lack of sexual energy (arousal), very little interest in intimacy (foreplay, sex, giving or receiving sexual pleasures), fear, insecurity, sense of unworthiness and shame are but a few symptoms of an unhealthy Root Chakra. While it is normal for people to experience some or all of these attributes depending upon external stimulation and inputs, if someone experiences any of these attributes for an extended period of time (based upon their normal personality) there may be a very serious imbalance in need of expeditious repair.

Often called the "Zest for Life" chakra, the Sacral Chakra represents the embodiment of warmth, radiance, friendliness and emotional stability. This chakra is your most important emotional center and everyone will experience an imbalance during their lifetime. This chakra is considered by some to be the center of women's sexual pleasure.

If the Root Chakra is healthy, the flow of energy will feed the Sacral Chakra enabling the intensity of the climax to increase. It may also cause the woman to have a very "quick and intense" orgasm with very little foreplay or other stimulation Many people practice yoga to keep their bodies in shape and the chakras open and healthy. More importantly, putting unhealthy emotions, people, and memories behind you is very important. If you cannot get past the mental barriers, no amount of work on the physical body will compensate. A healthy Sacral Chakra will usually be energetic, eager for life, enjoy their sexuality without having it rule them, be expressive, experience joy, be spontaneous and open to change. A Blockage may bring jealousy, betrayal, control and power plays.

"While demons often deliver your desires to the person and / or object of your magical focus, it is the all-important connection between energy and magic that serves as the mandatory process step for successful magical operations including spells, curses, conjuration and invocations. It's the dormant energy that rests at the base of the spine waiting for the chakras to align in harmony to awaken it."

"Just as chakras can have a negative impact on your health, conversely, your health can have a negative impact on your chakras. The two are closely interrelated and salubrious approach is a must for serious practitioners. A person must be dedicated to the principles of learning magic in order to become proficient. The association and connection between magical operations and the chakras is very relevant and important because without the health of the chakras, you will harm yourself much more while attempting magical rituals."

The nervous system and digestive system, including the liver, gall bladder, pancreas and spleen, are associated with the third chakra called the Solar Plexus. Concurrently, the Solar Plexus chakra allows you to really "know yourself", allowing you to determine your limitations. This chakra is also the key to emotional stability, inner peace, self-esteem and self-control. A person's willpower is directly linked to this "yellow chakra" and for those of you beginning a journey, starting over, cleaning out the 'closet of past chaos', this is the chakra that will need a great deal of your attention going forward.

Intuition and instincts are byproducts of repeated molding, shaping and strengthening of the Solar Plexus chakra. For this reason, Friedrich Nietzsche was correct; "What doesn't kill you, only makes you stronger". As you chisel this chakra into a work of art, you often will ask yourself "Am I going to die soon?" however, successful efforts result in a "regenerative id, an instinctive psyche and a higher intelligence plane". Some philosophically refer to this chakra as the ego however, I believe the ego has more than one chakra input.

Development of this chakra is also the first step to becoming a Cognitive Warrior; agile, dexterous, perspicacious, skillful and dangerous for anyone making a fatal mistake of underestimating you as an opponent. These traits, combined with the power of Satanic Magic, creates a force of nature that only tireless dedication, study and practice produce.

Many perceived altercations are ended within seconds as your opponent hits you with their idea of a "cognitive roundhouse punch". You will calmly open the gates of retribution and symbolically split their skull with your verbal spiked Mace!! They will have had only a glimpse of the power you command and they will flee as fast as possible to avoid the full load of your blitzkrieg attack. No one wants to appear stupid in the presence of their peers.

The next in line is named Anahata in Sanskrit........it is the Heart Chakra and represents "love"; not so fast, because everything that comes with love is not always pleasant. While everyone reading this can probably remember their First Love from many years ago (or maybe recently), they will probably also remember the sharp stinging in the chest caused by the end of that very special experience.

My fond memories are of innocence and naive exploration into the unknown; holding hands in the movie theatre, building the courage to put my arm around her shoulder and the sweet acceptance as she moved closer to snuggle with me.

Then, in the blink of an eye, she moved away and I never saw her again; my heart still reminds me of the sharp pain I experienced for the first time in my life that summer. I was totally unprepared and without the coping skills developed later, I was alone and truly broken-hearted.

As illustrated, you should be aware of the "pleasure and pain" aspects of this chakra. Grief, pain, anxiety and even fear are produced during the course of a normal week, day, hour or minute. In the fluid environment where tangibles are few and far between, the Heart Chakra must be developed to the point that nothing will bring it to a figurative or literal stop. Resilience will be developed over time while inputs from "healthy" Root, Sacral and Solar Chakras serve to nourish the Heart Chakra.

For Satanists, there is an added emphasis placed upon the proper development of this chakra with predominantly one primary reason: Self and the love of Self is a most important aspect of Satanic life.

This is another stage where more "personal baggage" must be acknowledged and dealt with properly in order to build the necessary foundation. While scar tissue may (and often does) remain, the importance of guilt acknowledgement and proper mitigation can not be overstated. Without proper treatment, the injury will return, over and over, to cause disruption, upheaval, pain, shame and embarrassment which results in..............GUILT! It is a vicious, festering cycle that will ultimately destroy a person from the inside out.

The heart plays a key role in many of the body's biological functions while serving vital roles in the emotional system and subsystems of a person's life. The heart also utilizes small electrical currents which not only send the signal to the heart to "beat" but it also sets the appropriate rhythm needed to ensure the needs of the body are met, whether sitting on the sofa or jogging down a sidewalk. It is ironic and terrifying at the same time to realize we are all one heartbeat away from death. That fact is very hard for some people to handle however, the Satanist views this philosophical "edge of the cliff" as just another event that occurs daily in the animal kingdom.

Frequently referred to as the "Fifth Chakra", Vissudha is the Sanskrit name for the Throat Chakra. Located in the throat area (jaw and neck area), this chakra is represented by the color turquoise and is utilized for creative self-expression of your "truths", which is sometimes very confusing for Satanists. Our belief discourages lies and lying however, Satanists acknowledge the fact that everyone lies from time to time AND there are consequences for lying that has nothing to do with 'right or wrong moral BS' and has a purely humanistic rationale.

When you lie, this opens a chasm in your aura which must be filled to close. Since you have practically set these sound vibrations free in a vast vacuum, a mystic venturi effect and just like a cut can become infected by germs, your aura may be impregnated by many things you do not want: DO NOT NEED in your life, period. More on this topic in other posts.

The Throat Chakra truths also extends to the delivery of your truths; your comfort level and effectiveness while revealing your truths. Some symptoms include stretching the truth for personal gain, shyness, anxiety or overwhelming fear of expression when sharing your truths. When out of balance, the use of any natural expressions you may have been gifted with become mechanical, forced and void of the feelings and sincerity with which you can easily deliver at any given time. Everything seems to be a daunting task that requires almost all of your energy to convey. Your natural abilities melt away and none of your "old tricks" can help. You are on an imaginary, yet very real, slippery slope to failure.

Vissudha means purification and that is the essence of truthfulness. If you are true to yourself, you will be able to use that truth as you express your real "self" to others. Singing, dancing and other forms of communication allow for better expression of the Self.

It has been said "Perception is reality". This chakra is the key to the "self perception". Through this sixth chakra known as Ajna (to command), a Satanist can master the mind and begin focusing energy as they wish. The third eye allows us to have a clear perception of our reality so we can fully understand our purpose in life. Legitimate Fortune Tellers, Palm Readers and Clairvoyants have been known to use this 'second sight' chakra which allows auras, colors and images to be seen using Extrasensory Perception (ESP). Located between the eyebrows, this indigo colored chakra it is thought to be connected to the pineal gland. It is the link between the inner and out worlds.

Intuition and intuitive perception processes are only part of the potential benefits. Many artists, writers, musicians, etc. often experience the immediate and spontaneous "idea"; which is certainly a byproduct of an open Third Eye. Visualization and the ability to use the imagination to formulate an intuitive abstract solution to a theoretical problem or situation.

Blocks in this chakra cause us to become delusional, unimaginative, indifferent and to have poor memories. Worry is a big problem, spaced-out, and poor concentration also plague a person with a sickly, unhealthy third eye chakra.

To the Satanist, developing the Third Eye is the most important chakra to develop. Without it, the Satanist will never enter the true Satanic realm. Perhaps the atheists calling themselves "Satanists" should devote some time and energy to this chakra.

"Synchronicity is the coming together of inner and outer events in a way that cannot be explained by cause and effect... and that is meaningful to the observer."Carl Jung

The "Thousand-Petaled Lotus" (aka Crown Chakra) is located at the top of the head, in the brain. The actual purpose and uses of this chakra is sometimes highly debated by religious gurus, self-improvement enthusiasts, Macroprospectus experts, Yoga instructors and students of metaphysical spirituality. Why? Anytime the question of a "higher being" comes up, folks are ready for all hell to break loose.

The Sekhem (power / force) is the aura of spirituality and the innate human belief of "someone / something of a divine nature". This chakra works in concert with the Ajna and some believe these two chakras are all that remains of our being after death. The energy remaining penetrates other dimensional worlds from the Crown Chakra; the human body joining the earth through the inevitable process of decay.

The Sahasara (a sustainment of thousand) combines intellect with belief, emotion, intuition (from the Third Eye), visualization, reason, imagination and frustration due to physical limitation. The "tug of war" behind the scenes often tilts the scales of sanity; resulting in confusion, detachment, illusions and delusion. For those who believe the development of this chakra involves buying a yoga mat, I hate to burst your bubble. Yoga means "union" or"discipline." It's great for exercise and it will help by releasing energy through exertion and increasing mental focus however, it is not a requirement for development of the chakras. A lack of understanding results in 1) nothing beyond the physical or 2) a total mental breakdown.

Satanic Magic is a blend of many things; past, present, future; organic and manufactured; good and bad; noise and silence; etc. There are many ingredients that are blended in order to produce magic and development of the inner-self and chakras only represents part of the equation. The recipe for magical success not only requires the proper ingredients, but the mixture must be balanced in the correct proportions.

Just as medieval Alchemists tirelessly searched for the "golden formula", a Satanist must always push the limits of experimentation and magical practice in order to reap the benefits. In your magical pursuits, be sure to develop the chakras while concurrently developing your magical abilities. Do not be satisfied when scratching the surface of Satanic Magic. Strengthening your chakras takes time and energy however, the return on investment will exceed your wildest expectations!

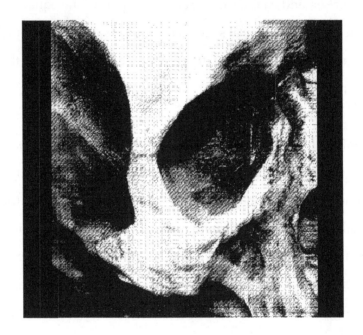

The Warrior

"In the absence of willpower the most complete collection of virtues and talents is wholly worthless." Aleister Crowley

Willpower causes theory to render results and without the action of willpower, ideas become dormant, dying thoughts. No amount of hope, suggestion or utterances will transform the abstract into the physical. Those who wait for someone else to perform the work will certainly not be invited to share the fruits of that labor.

The transfer of energy from person to inanimate object has been taught in many belief systems. Objects do not possess significant power or energy however, the Satanist can transfer energy created during ritual to an object; thus making the object an extension of the Satanist's energy.

The Japanese teach this principle in *Iaido*. This martial art teaches control of the Japanese sword in motions such as drawing, striking, clearing the opponent's blood from the blade (through motion) and replacing the sword in the *Saya* (scabbard or sheath).

One main concept in Iaido focuses on using the blade as an extension of the whole person - not only the arm but the life energy produced deep within the warrior. This force in the Japanese language is called *Ki*. The life force is also recognized by other nationalities, arts and practices however, the meaning remains the same.

There is a point to be made in this discussion. Ancient belief systems have known (and used) the unseen powers available to humans since the beginning of time yet, people in the *"West"* dismiss the true power of the forces because they require time, attention and practice to fully cultivate and control. As a society, the West desires *"drive through"* magical development.

In countless martial arts practice halls (Dojo) around the world, practitioners of all arts invest of themselves in order to recoup their investment with knowledge and ultimately, power. Those who enter the Dojo to learn how to "hurt someone" are soon invited to "readjust their objectives" or "kindly leave". The reason: one person can poison the entire group's energy resulting in the group's collective failure to laster their chosen craft.

Those entering the art for the therapeutic, spiritual and health benefits learn to defend themselves as a byproduct....it is a benefit of the hard work however, it is not the prime objective. Who would believe Tai Chi could actually be deadly?

Satanism is similar; since Satanic Magic can seriously hurt someone. If that is the reason for learning Satanism, the seeker will soon loose interest and become frustrated, even angry, sowing the seeds of discourse and negativity throughout the coven. He / she wants MORE; they want action and immediate results.

I have had the displeasure of ejecting quite a few of these Trouble-makers from my virtual Satanic Forum and Chatroom. It becomes tiring to deal with these imbeciles day after day, which is precisely the reason I delayed creating a forum for so long. In the end, I believe dedicated searchers receive a value from having a safe and respectful place to learn and share ideas about Satanism and the Occult Arts. I invest the time to ensure the environment remains safe.

As with any worthwhile endeavor, Satanism requires investment and full dedication of mind, spirit and body. If you learn Satanism as an art form, magic will be realized as a benefit; not the single focus of the practice. If someone wants to learn magic tricks, go to a school of magic, not a Satanic coven. Not only is the petty whining and complaining a detractor to everyone else in the group, it is also a health risk. The "straw that broke the camel's back" is a heavy load that may not end well for the *Trouble-maker! Finis!*

The Coven

For any magical operation, energy creation and energy control are the most important factors. Whether crossing a dimensional chasm or going about the *Devil's Work*, energy accomplishes the desired tasks. The practitioner may be reciting dead, *dogma-laden* poetry, with no hope of his / her desires being met, if the understanding of energy creation, control and dissipation (for the health of those involved) has been lost or never acquired in the beginning.

The gaze of the *Third Eye* can actually reveal the motive of a practitioner. Mastery of this element is very challenging for those who are not born with the natural ability. A full discussion of this topic would certainly require no less than a book dedicated entirely to an in-depth analysis of methodologies. The subject matter demands exhaustive research and understanding. It is considered a Higher Magic process closely associated with chakra development.

Since individuals are sometimes blessed with occult "gifts", there is much to be said concerning the formation and composition of the Satanic coven. As with any endeavor, finding the right skill set is critical to practical success. The skills must complement one another, leverage the strengths while mitigating risks resulting from individual (or group) weaknesses. The composition of the coven will play a vital role in the overall success of the Higher Magic processes. Much thought and planning should go into the clear path of the coven.

Personalities of coven members is an important Higher Magic element that will determine future success or failure. While any group will undergo the stages of team formation, growth, engagement, work product and (as with most) dissolving of the group, it is important to choose the thirteen members (or *twenty-six*) wisely while clearly identifying the members' strengths and weaknesses. I recommend the use of a SWOT Analysis during this process.

Early on, the coven should decide in what area(s) of magic the group aspires to become proficient and set a clear objective (including the path) for achieving the objective. Far reaching challenges are great for an established coven, operating at or near peak proficiency / efficiency however, the newly formed coven should be realistic and set objectives that perhaps *"roll up into"* an overall challenging objective. Be realistic and remain grounded, realizing there will be many other challenges for the fledgling coven.

The psychological effect of achieving an objective can not be overstated. For a new coven, achieving a few small objectives early on will build camaraderie, improve individual confidence, bond the members together and identify weaknesses that can easily be mitigated without detracting from the group's productivity.

The mental benefits are intangible (yet required) elements that send a resounding positive energy effect rippling through the coven. Everyone wants to be part of the winning team......never forget that important concept.

The Leader (official or unofficial) of the coven will require a specialized set of skills that many people *"believe they possess"* however, the coven must look past the subjective opinions and evaluate the true abilities and proficiencies. The success of the coven greatly depends upon this vital step.

This subject may very well <u>end the coven</u> before it begins, since many people with differing motives, egos and ideas must unanimously agree upon who will lead the coven. The decision itself is only the beginning and any member with "hurt feelings" can sow the seeds of discourse; ensuring the future fracture or demise of the coven. This important point can (*and often does*) destroy the foundation of the group. Difficult decisions require responsibility and resolve. The Leader must lead and it will not always be easy or a great joy to execute the duties of the office.

The coven leader will have a daunting path ahead of him / her. There must be a clear understanding of this role in the holistic aspect. The position requires a diverse set of "people skills" due to the nucleus-type position. Soft skills can be developed however, the person must have the natural abilities to build upon. Conflict resolver, negotiator, enforcer, provider, protector, educator, servant, coordinator, speaker, organizer, judge, magician, confidant, praetorian cohort, planner.............just to name a few.

The Leader must also know and understand his / her own limitations; including emotional, sexual, mental and physical. Setting a proper pace and cadence for the coven will help level the peaks, valleys and overall level of effort. A person may be a fantastic Leader however, no one benefits if he / she becomes *"burned out"* in the first six months of service. For the ambitious Leader, this is a very real possibility.

A *Word of Warning* to the Sole Practitioner...... If you are a solitary practicing Satanist, the idea of joining a coven may be enticing however, **not all that glimmers is gold**! Joining a coven is not required. Desperation leads to fatal mistakes.

As discussed herein, the term Satanism is tossed around quite often and not all that meets the eye is true. I have heard horror stories from survivors of rape, assault, robbery, identity theft and other vicious crimes that have happened to those searching for a coven to join. I have also heard of human trafficking groups that were under a guise of Satanic coven. Be careful! Not everyone is searching for the same enlightenment. Use common sense although it is not so common.

Countless people email me weekly to ask for advice or a recommendation of a coven in their area. I caution each and every one to be careful and never trust strangers......never go to a secluded location with someone unless you have others (friends you trust) with you. Do not rush or be intimidated through ultimatums.......simply walk (or run) away!

Be smart and never continue a situation that makes you uncomfortable. Never feel intimidated or prohibited from contacting law enforcement to report illegal activities.

If you believe illegal activities are involved, extricate yourself, go to a safe place and notify law enforcement immediately. *Satanism gives no one a right or approval to break the law!* Any coven that promotes, advocates, requires or allows such activities to occur (through empathy or other means) **is not, I REPEAT, is not** practicing real Satanic Magic or any form of true Satanism. Cults have attempted to serve their own purposes by making new members perform illegal activities and later, using those activities to force or coerce (through blackmail) the new members into sex slavery or other acts.

Silentium In Persona Diaboli

"No, I am not a satanist. I am a pagan. Satanism is another thing."
Kenneth Anger

I received a grimoire entitled *Silentium In Persona Diaboli* during my trip to Germany over Xmas and New Year 2012 / 2013. My *Patriarchal Coven* presides in Germany (Bavaria to be precise) and has been a major influence for my magic and teachings in the USA and around the world. I will use excerpts from the grimoire in the and future volumes of Sanctum of Shadows. I feel the information contained therein is as powerful, useful and relevant today as when first recorded many decades ago. There are many lessons to be learned from the scholarly, mystical passages.

The original grimoire manuscript was written (circa) the late 1400s. The copy I received was reproduced in 1962. The informal *"Introduction"* (Front Matter) references the first Spanish *auto-da-fé* in Seville, Spain. This event took place (circa) 1481 which provides a plausible baseline supporting the hypotheses of those who, in the past, have examined the original and declared it *"valid and authentic"*. The **Quemadero De Tablada** is mentioned as a 'tongue in cheek' slur at face value. After reading the entire section (five pages), it seems to be a very personal attack on the insanity that was gripping Europe as the Inquisition went into "overdrive". There is a "Gefühl" of impending death that resonates within the pages.

The six canons in the grimoire are collectively called **Profunditas Caecitas.** These canons are similar to a *"witches' code"* that directs members of the coven in general terms. In my opinion, the *Profunditas Caecitas* provides guidance to perhaps new initiates and new members of a coven. The mention of specific events suggests the book was a "work in progress", actually requiring at least a decade to complete.

The text is distinctive as reproduced from the original book. It is written in German however, the dialect is predominantly Bavarian with a sparse peppering of *Schwäbisch* words and distinctive phrases that currently exist from the Stuttgart to the Augsburg area. There is also unwritten folklore that has been passed from generation to generation.

The important thing about this grimoire is an illustration of how powerful a grimoire can truly become. The diligent scribes who recorded the works did a fantastic job of capturing the subtleties of their rituals and general thoughts on the subject of magic. Each page is filled with emotion and enthusiasm which speaks volumes of the dedications and devotion of those early practitioners.

The book does not credit an author however, during my discussions in December 2012, I learned that it is commonly believed the grimoire was assembled from the workings of an entire thirteen member Witch's Coven, with each member contributing works from 'literal lifetimes' of passing information through lineage and persistent practice.

The output of such dedication and devotion is a book of magical knowledge, obedience and meticulous transcription. In our *"drive through"* society, it represents a testament to patience, persistence and diligence.

After the book was completed, it is said to have traveled throughout Germany, Austria, Italy, Poland, France and Prussia; surfacing just before 1740 during the annexation of Silesia by *"King Frederick II The Great of Prussia"*. From Silesia, the book surfaced one final time before World War II (1926) in Katowice Voivodeship. It is rumored (yet unverified) that the grimoire spent time at the infamous **Wewelsburg Castle** under direct control of SS Commander *Heinrich Himmler*. As the fortunes of war turned against Germany, Himmler attempted to destroy the castle and the grimoire disappeared for the decades after the war. The book was purchased during a sale in München (1961) and has been 'home' with the coven ever since. Before leaving Germany, we performed a ritual to keep the blessings and demonic forces intact while transporting the reproduced manuscript to my home in Florida.

The *Crone* of the coven provided very valuable insight and explained many of the language features particularly, the fact that in the old German language, when the grimoire was written, everyone used a *"third person"* tense; written and spoken. This is a key point and was pivotal to a correct understanding of the text. She also shared some points that I feel must be passed along to you.......the reader and Satanist. In the next chapter of this book, together **you and I will take part in furthering the precious revived messages**.

Just as I earlier suggested to you (to perform a ritual and ask for understanding from Satan), I too asked for Satanic guidance and special demonic insight before reading the grimoire. After reading the entire book twice, over the period of a month, I began decomposing the text, forming a plausible interpretation, translated into English and reduced it to written form.

During the process, I experienced several *demonic - induced* visions as I worked on certain sections of the text. Without those inducements, I do not believe I would have fully understood (or appreciated) the messages that were being communicated. If you followed my instructions, I believe you too will experience such inducements as you read the volumes.

Even now, as I read those passages, I know there was a gentle Satanic hand guiding the original author and I am also very confident there was Satanic guidance helping me during my translation so the integrity and aesthetic impact would neither be diluted nor lost.

This book has energy and life. One day in the future, when Aleister Nacht has been permanently installed as a member of Satan's most high court, the Hosts of Hell, perhaps someone will take my translation of *Silentium In Persona Diaboli*, call upon our Master Satan and once again renew the grimoire to share with other Satanists of the future. It is my sincere desire to continue furthering His message long after my dimensional crossover. Hail Satan! So mote it be!

Wichtige Absätze

I have selected special passages to share with you from the grimoire *Silentium In Persona Diaboli*. These items were picked for their merit and the point conveyed by the author.

I will include the text as originally written, my interpretation of the text as provided by my Demonic Familiar, followed by my interpretation and *"take away"* of the point.

"Vom Licht in die Dunkelheit auf dem Pfad des kleinsten Wiederstandes reist unsere Kraft. Es ist wichtig für die Hexe dieses Konzept zu verstehen."

"From light to darkness, energy travels the path of least resistance. It is important for the Witch to understand this concept."

This simple, yet profound, statement was made in *Profunditas Caecitas;* the section containing the six canons. To the casual reader, this is nothing more than an inordinate axiom however, the Satanist grasps the meaning more deeply.

Energy inherently flows from areas of surfeit to vacuums or *voids*. Energy mimics liquids, gases and fluids (air has the same characteristic as well) by "rushing into" the space, creating force, speed and volume during the process. If you create the void, energy will naturally *"attempt to fill"* the area, space or thing. I can almost imagine most reader's lightbulb coming on as the implications and applications of this simple property of physics is grasped and understood.

"Einklang im Hexenzirkel ist ein Gebot für wirkungsvolle Magie."

"Harmony within the coven is a requirement for effective magic."

This simple concept has been mentioned earlier in this book however, it is worth re-mentioning for obvious reasons. During 25+ years of studying the occult, I have not seen real, factual evidence of *Chaos Magic*. Perhaps I have not witnessed the right coven however, I have never seen a magical working result from chaos.

More than mere chaos, this statement goes the the root of the matter and attacks those who constantly create trouble and turmoil within the coven. I have pretty much flogged that subject in this book so I will cease and desist. Those knuckle-dragging idiots that will never grasp true magic, simply want to destroy and eradicate. Eject them immediately from your coven!

"Glaube ans Unglaudliche. Dies ist eine Voraussetzung um magische Kraft zu steuern."

"Believe in the unbelievable. This is a prerequisite of energy control."

Earlier in this book I explained why this is important however, it is worth a quick review. While skepticism is acceptable and healthy, many seekers condemn their magical practice to failure because they can not go over the hurdle that is *"Doubt"*. Believe and you <u>*will*</u> achieve.

Everyone must decide what is true and plausible for them however, be aware of the ***"Paralysis of Analysis"*** syndrome (not actually a medical syndrome). Some people refer to this as the *"over-thinking"* condition.

A person can easily talk them self out of what initially seemed a rational and intelligent theory. Consider all information at hand, evaluate the alternatives and go. This concept follows the same guideline. If you do not believe magic is real and powerful, you are doomed to failure. It is that simple...........

"Ordnung ist der Stamm einer gut geführten Gruppe. Caos züchtet Coas und Zerrüttung des Zirkels."

"Order is the root of a well managed group. Disorder breeds disorder and fragmentation of the coven."

See the last explanation which covers this statement nicely. Again, chaos is not magic.

"Die Jenigen die nur nehmen ohne zu geben zerstören den Kreis. Jedes Mitglied muss geben um den Erfolg der Gruppe zu garantieren."

"Those who take without giving shall destroy the coven. Every member must donate to the success of the group."

This statement aligns nicely with Anton LaVey's explanation of a *Psychic Vampire*:

> *"Many people who walk the earth practice the fine art of making others feel responsible and even indebted to them, without cause. Satanism observes these leeches in their true light. Psychic vampires are individuals who drain others of their vital energy. This type of person can be found in all avenues of society. They fill no useful purpose in our lives, and are neither love objects nor true friends. Yet we feel responsible to the psychic vampire without knowing why."*
>
> The Satanic Bible by Anton LaVey

Anton's point should be well taken by all Satanists and coven members. Those "leeches" will certainly drain the energy from the group however, applying the lessons of this chapter we know energy actually flows *toward* these individuals. Those members will drain your magical energy.

"Disziplin in dem Kreis muss schnell und stark ausgeführt werden Erlaube niemals die Ausbreitung einer Infektion des Zirkels. Süsses Obst soll an die Tiere des Waldes gefüttert werden."

"Discipline in the coven must be fast, firm and decisive. Never allow an infection to spread within the coven. Good fruit should be savored while bitter fruit should be fed to the animals of the forest."

As I wrote earlier in the book, those individuals who can not *"get with the program"* and abide by the established norms of the coven should soon find they are without a group. The longer the *"wound"* is allowed to fester, the more painful and dangerous the infection becomes.

I am not advocating hast; evaluate the problem and discuss the best possible solutions with the other coven members however, once the plan of action has been established, be decisive and surgical. Remove the member and any reminders of his / her presence quickly and cleanly. **NOTE:** A scalpel removes a cancer much better than denial, pleading or a *"butter knife"*. Some people only understand savage brutality. A course correction for the coven may require a healthy dose of this medicine!

"Die jenigen die einem Mitglied des Kreises Unheil zufügen, sollen sofort bestraft werden."

"Those who hurt a member of the coven shall receive the correction immediately!"

See the translations above. *"Immediately"* is the keyword to this passage.

"Der Altar ist am wichtigsten und ist der Mittelpunkt des Zirkels."

"The Altar is most important. It is the center of the coven."

The importance and significance of the Altar is pointed out in this excerpt. This is significant for several reasons (practicality, metaphorically, realistically, etc.) however, I will also share the Crone's explanation and thoughts on this matter.

During the time *Silentium In Persona Diaboli* was written, it has been said the normal orientation of a coven's sanctum differed from that of modern times. The availability of meeting areas, the ritual to be performed and other factors determined where the coven met and what the physical limits of the meeting area would be.

In towns and villages, the ground floor of a building often served as a stable (*barn*) for the building's residents. Most had a similar appearance to the vaulted sections of ceiling found in a cavern or wine cellar. **Note:** To visualize this concept, Google a picture of the Beetles playing the Liverpool Cavern Club. The vaults of the ceiling are very distinguishable.

These buildings would have several "apartment" style living spaces that squeezed every square centimeter of space out of the utilized area. For the coven, space for ritual work was at a premium and so the members adjusted to accommodate.

It was customary for the ritual altar to be in the middle of a room with coven members surrounding the altar in a circle. You may have noticed the German word *Zirkels* in the text excerpts. The coven was often referred to as the *"Circle"*. The word *"Coven"* originated in the 1500s; almost 100 years after **Silentium In Persona Diaboli** was written. The placement of the altar placed against a wall of the sanctum came much later.

"Scham ist eine menschliche Kreation und hat deshalb keinen Platz im Kreise."

"Shame is a human creation. It has no place in the coven."

Martin Luther's *reform movement* began (circa) 1517 when his collection of thoughts, ideas and thesis (of his beliefs) was published. His excommunication from the Catholic church came later in 1521. Before the early 1500s, there had been an absence of *"self-righteousness"* throughout Germany and Austria. For example, nudity was not viewed as being anything other than *"natural"*. With the reform movement came baseless *"shame"* for being human. This theology thrives even in modern society.

The *"shame"* mentioned in **Silentium In Persona Diaboli** referred to actions sometimes employed by the coven during rituals such as *"Sex Magic"*. It was understood by the members that certain actions must happen in order to fulfill the creation and accumulation of energy for success. As one can imagine, a Sex Ritual requires some sexual stimulation in order to generate the needed energy.

No member of the coven should bear shame, degradation or humiliation for contributing to any ritual or magical working. Many rituals of this type were held around the time of *Fasching (Shrovetide)*, and although covens did not celebrate, they certainly took advantage of dressing up and wearing masks in the traditional fashion. Wearing a disguise enabled the members to move about and where larger numbers of average citizens congregated, Sex Rituals often took place with no one noticing due to the celebratory atmosphere and vast number of people congregated into small, dense areas.

"Magie ist der Anlass für den Hexenzirkel. Dieser Zirkel ist der Grundstein für Magie aber nicht der einzige Bestandteil. Der Kreis möge sich ändern, die Magie bleibt immer gleich.......immer."

"Magic is the reason for the coven. The coven is an element of magic but never to be the only element. The coven may change but the magic remains the same......always!"

This statement illustrates the importance of maintaining order and the hierarchy of importance concerning magic. Magic is the *all important* reason and everything else is meant to accompany, supplement or accent magic; not the other way around.

This also fits nicely this way: *"Satan is the reason for Satanism. Without Satan, there is no Satanism!"*

Vampirism

Anton LaVey's characterization of a "vampire" was totally fugitively presented as someone who would certainly drain the life from anyone who was willing to allow the vampire to sink his / her teeth into them. There are however, real vampires among us in this reality. They are real; just as a leech feeds upon blood, they too hunger for the life-sustaining plasma from which life flows.

As pointed out earlier in this book, I have seen things that are extremely difficult to verbalize, explain or (at times) comprehend. The phenomena of Vampirism is precisely one of those aspects that, for the chicken-hearted, should remain *"unsaid"*.

I am not an expert on the subject of vampirism nor do I claim to know much more than the average occult student however, I have had occasion to witness a limited number of events that I categorize as "vampiric" in nature.

My very first experience with vampirism was many, many years ago in California. It was my first trip as a new coven member and we were camping in the Ojai Valley in preparation for the Summer Solstice Ritual.

This commune-style campground was a *"hippie heaven"* complete with plenty weed, spray painted cars, trucks and the legendary Volkswagen (VW) van.

The attendees of this celebration made up an eclectic group of Satanists (mostly Devil Worshipers), Wiccan and many other forms of the Occult Arts. The early 1980s were fantastic and I always remember the good things that happened; not the bad things that came later in that decade. I was quite familiar with blood rituals however, I had never experienced *Vampirism*.

During the ritual, members of two coven groups domiciled near Los Angeles practiced vampirism. The blood was "donated" by two dedicated members. During the ritual, an athame was used to make a small incision across the wrist. This technique (I later learned) enabled a good flow without clotting or the possibility of a wound being too deep or wide. When a person attempts suicide, he / she usually makes the cut parallel with the arm; not across it, for this very reason.

The blood was collected in a chalice and passed around their semicircle where they stood. This was before the extensive knowledge society now possesses concerning the dangers of blood borne pathogens and diseases. I even considered trying it with them but, I lost my nerve and *"chickened-out"*. I could not get past the salty-iron smell of the warm blood-filled chalice.

During that week of festivities, I was able to discuss the meaning and methods the coven had used for many years and I remember an interesting statement made by one of the coven members when I asked *"Why do you do it? What does it mean to you personally?"* The answer: *"To drink the blood of a brother or sister brings us closer together; physically and mentally. We are able to share the energy held in the blood and release it during the ritual performed during that time."*

While taking blood from someone (or even yourself) may be more than you are willing to do for whatever the reason(s), if the member has accepted the idea and moved beyond the sickly, sinking feeling of the stomach, the idea does not seem so foreign compared to other events that happen during and after rituals.

As for me, I have never tasted another person's blood and I do not intend to do so. This is personal preference and has nothing to do with the performance of any ritual. It is not required in our coven and, as far as I can tell, the omission of this element has no adverse effects or limiting factors on the results of our rituals.

Meditation

NOTE: Consult a healthcare professional prior to beginning any exercise program including the breathing exercises in this book.

There are several exercises that are very beneficial for the Satanist wishing to practice meditation. Each one of these exercises is designed to rejuvenate a certain aspect, more especially, the Chakras of the Satanist.

Satanic meditation is very important. For most people, meditation is just something that you may want to do as a hobby. For the Satanist, meditation is very important on a daily basis for the Satanic Spirit while it rejuvenates the mind and the body.

The Chakras, which I discussed earlier in this book, are the individual centers that direct energy from the lowest point of the body, all the way through to the highest point of the body. When energized, the Chakras begin to rotate or spin. The health of the chakras is very important to the Satanist.

Keeping the Chakras clear in order to promote the flow of energy is very, very important. If a Chakra becomes block, the energy cannot flow naturally and when the energy cannot flow naturally, there are adverse effects that take place in the body, mind and spirit. These three elements are joined very closely together and because the body is connected closely with the mind and spirit, each one dramatically effects the others elements.

Performing these exercises will certainly improve your meditation technique and improve your health through the exercise of using your Chakras. One example of this exercise is to inhale and exhale deeply and / or at varying speeds or cadences. While this sounds very elementary, it actually requires some thought and concentration.

The idea in this first exercise is to imagine a thin rope or string; as you **inhale** through the nostrils, imagine the rope or string flowing in through your nose and coiling around in the lower abdomen. Hold the breath for 10 seconds then slowly and in a controlled manner, **exhale** through the mouth.

Do not hold your breath when you exhale; go right back into your next inhale breathing repetition; in through the nose, imagining the rope coiling in the lower abdomen. Hold your breath for 10 seconds and then exhale through the mouth. Repeat this exercise numerous times.

While performing this exercise over the period of say, five minutes, you are actually rejuvenating your body by reducing the amount of CO_2 (*Carbon Dioxide*) and harmful toxins that may be in your bloodstream. The objective is to release that CO_2 and harmful toxins from the bloodstream, with an exchange through the lungs as you exhale. By doing this, you will feed the brain fresh *oxygen-rich* air enabling you to think more clearly. This technique is wonderful for relieving stress. Those practicing Vampirism, will find this exercise useful to cleanse the blood before ingestion.

We live with stress every day and our world is a busy, fast-paced society. This exercise is designed to slow the body's metabolism by slowing the heart rate through controlled breathing. You can almost feel the stress leaving your body during each exhale. Five minutes of this exercise will significantly reduce your stress level. Clarity and a "free feeling" is a byproduct of this exercise which most Satanists will find almost *addictive*.

The second exercise that I feel is very beneficial to the Satanist is called *"Separation Breath"*. This breathing technique is different from the first because this technique uses a more rapid repetition with exhaled breaths. The only time you hold your breath, is for five seconds at the end of the exhale. There is also a more "forced" exhalation as opposed to a smooth exhale.

Breathe in with a *quick breath* until you feel your lungs are full (but not filled to capacity) with air. Do not hold your breath at the top of the inhale; when you begin to feel tightness in your lungs, immediately begin exhaling quickly and with deliberate force. You should try to push the air from your lungs as quickly as humanly possibly.

When you have exhaled all of the air and you feel the slight discomfort, hold your breath for five seconds. You do not want to totally deflate your lungs; that is not what you are trying to do with this exercise however, you *are* trying to exhale a large amount of air. Hold your breath for five seconds at the bottom of the exhale, then inhale quickly. Repeat this exercise for five minutes.

Before we go any further with exercises, now that I have introduced some breathing techniques, let us discuss what your mind is going to be doing during these exercises. As you are incorporating these breathing techniques, you want to control your mind. Exercise of your brain is important to its development and maintenance.

I recommend thinking about something that really, really makes you happy or satisfied. You want to go to your metaphorical *"happy place"* by controlling your mind and going to that area that you frequently enjoy. You will notice I am not saying *"clear your mind"*; that has been proven impossible for the human mind. You are essentially taking your mind out of gear, putting it in neutral or idling the mind while forcing your thoughts to be the ones you want to use.

By using these exercises, you are going to really decrease your stress level. You will also prepare your mind, spirit and body for the acceptance of those things which cannot be explained in the physical world. As discussed earlier, if you practice Satanism long enough, you will experience some things that simply cannot be explained or comprehended by the untrained mind.

In Satanism, we must open our minds and we must be aware *and ready* to accept those things of which no explanation exists. Clearing the mind, spirit and body through these two exercises is a wonderful way to start any Satanic ritual or other working. You must prepare your mind to accept what you are about to behold. Meditation is also very important *after* a ritual working or other Satanic practice. By clearing your Chakras after you have performed a ritual, you will certainly realize the advantage and remain cognitively healthy.

I'll remind you that the last thing you should do when you finish a ritual is to grab your grimoire and write down your experiences. I cannot stress this enough for the Satanist. After a magical working, I will sometimes perform a breathing exercise and then write my experiences and thoughts in my grimoire. I find that by using this sequence, I am able to describe what I have witnessed and the events that have taken place. Clearing the body of the harmful toxins with breathing exercises is of great benefit. Wiccan practitioners sometimes mirror this decompression.

A third exercise I will share with you is a breathing technique that *combines* the slow inhale method with the rapid exhale resulting in a relaxed mind while you are forcing the CO_2 and harmful toxins from your lungs at a much faster rate.

The martial arts have used breathing techniques for centuries. Martial artists will breathe in and then breathe out quickly as they strike their opponent. This rapid exhale is called Ki (in Japanese) and actually adds power to their thrust or strike. I discussed this and the martial art of Iaido earlier in this book.

Athletes outside of martial arts studies use controlled breathing techniques in their field as well. One such example is weight lifting. The weight-lifter will inhale and as they are moving or lifting the weight, they will exhale using this technique. The rapid exhale actually increases their ability to move the weight. Again, breathing techniques can be very beneficial; mentally and physically.

For the sake of this topic, I would also like to add one thing about health in closing this chapter. It is important for the Satanist.......important for anyone, to take care of their body. We only have one body, one mind and one spirit and if we abuse those, especially the body, we will lose that precious gift that we have been given.

It is really *your choice* as to how to take care of your body. It is also important to recognize that things such as smoking is actually KILLING YOU by the minute.

Maintaining your body and mind and the ability to have a *quality of life* is very important. If you do not maintain your health, you will come to rely upon someone else to take care of you. Be responsible and take care of yourself. This begins by taking care of your body and not abusing it.

Many people have ruined their health with substances such as drugs, cigarettes, alcohol, fatty foods or not exercising. There is one way to ensure that you will be healthy: take care of yourself!! Satanism does not condemn a person for smoking however, if you truly love Satanism, you will want to enjoy Satanism as long as physically (and mentally) possible. Live a happy lifestyle and live a healthy lifestyle. It is the Satanist's choice however, you should *be responsible* and *take responsibility* for your actions. Do not waste your life. Take care of that which you have been given.

I was addicted to heroin and I wasted some of my health taking that drug. That is time I will never get back; it almost killed me.

Finding Satanism saved my life and I sincerely hope anyone reading this, who is struggling with addiction, will find Satanism to be that which will free them from the bondage of addiction.

Advice

I want to share five little tidbits of magical operation; some insider trading notes that may help save time and further the Satanic process for you. While I have littered this book with *magical concept* highlights that I feel are important, these six are based upon my experiences. Do not overlook the importance and possible impact these items can have simply because they sound quite elementary. The most simple things in the world can be the most challenging when viewed as individual elements. These six hypotheses are simple in theory yet will prove difficult in application. I assure you, many Satanists have wasted opportunities because these principles were not implemented and maintained over time.

I. *"Repetition sets a solid magical foundation that monotony will attempt to crack."* Some magical operations may be conducted numerous times without any noticeable result. Continuing this repetition requires concentration, tenacity, dedication and persistence. You are investing in a future return so remain focused and do not allow your actions to become thoughtless *"dogma"*. When you least expect it, Satan will swing wide the gates of knowledge and you will be plunged into that which you have so diligently pursued. At that moment, it will seem effortless.

II. *"Help only those who are serious about helping themselves."* Every day of the year, I receive email requesting my help. Many of these correspondences are from those who are in need of clarification or advice however, there are also those who want *"something for nothing"*. Everyone wishing to practice the Satanic Arts must do the work required. I will not pontificate on this point however, if you become drawn into the web of such a leech, he / she will consume your time without compensation, consideration or end. Invest in yourself! Those wanting a free ride will simply be left behind.

III. *"Remain within your capabilities and magical competence."* While self-explanatory, there is a difference between competence area, comfort zone and pushing your magical boundaries. Seek to balance opportunity with limitation, power with humility, safety with risk management and break down multifaceted concepts into manageable elements. Enjoy the triumphs then, resume the hard work!

IV. *"Do not become a prisoner of your own Valhalla."* Satanic rituals will be exciting and may become addictive to a new Satanist or Satanic coven. Sex rituals may quickly be the only events on the "Coven Calendar". A coven practicing only sexual-related activities will soon loose members, loose focus and degrade into a sex club. Variety is the spice of life. Always broaden your horizons.

V. *"Use all of your sense faculties to learn about Satanic Magic and <u>never</u> prematurely dismiss ideas or theories of others without proper due consideration."* As you become more and more proficient in magical operations, there will be a tendency to assert your knowledge and opinions concerning such subject matter. I caution you here; listen and consider every word, letter and sign before you. You will (should) always be a student of Satanism and as such, always willing and eager to look at things from different angles and perspectives. An answer or solution to a problem may be right in front of you...............do not overlook it. Seek to learn and learn to listen. Put the ego aside and you will develop personally as a Satanist.

VI. *"When managing the coven, develop those individuals who are motivated. 'Knowledgeable' does not necessarily equal motivation however, 'motivation' will certainly lead to increased knowledge."* As the leader of your coven, members will serve at your pleasure. Unless you wish to spend all of your time *"doing"* as opposed to *"managing"* the numerous tasks that are required, you should develop those members that have a desire to do the work. A motivated member will learn however, a knowledgeable member may or may not *"get the job done"*. Invest time in those who are willing to complete the work and are resourceful enough to solve problems to your satisfaction. Give praise when due and constructive criticism as needed. Discipline should be used as a "last resort" however, when needed, the correction should be fast and without any hesitation.

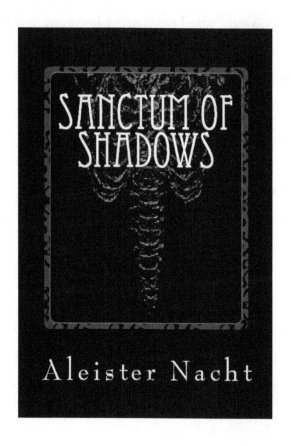

In Closing

Dear Searcher, Brother or Sister,

I sincerely hope you have found a benefit while reading my book. It is my desire to further Satanism as I truly believe it would make our world a better place in which to live. If you are interested in further advancement in the Black Arts, feel free to contact me. I have counseled hundreds of those Seekers wishing to find a solid footing in Satanism. You should expect to invest in such personalized guidance. Everyone needs a helping hand to achieve their goals and asking for help is not a sign of "weakness"; it demonstrates intelligence and a sincere intention to take the Satanic Arts *seriously*.

May the blessings of Hell pour upon you and provide you with your desires. I would like to hear from you. Write to me at aleisternacht@rocketmail.com or visit my website at www.AleisterNacht.com.

Aleister Nacht

A~N

Glossary

Athame - A double-edged ritual knife used in modern Witchcraft and Satanism.

Auric - Of or relating to the aura supposedly surrounding a living creature.

Auto-da-fé - The ritual of public penance of condemned heretics and apostates.

Baphomet - Baphomet (/ˈbæfəmɛt/; from medieval Latin Baphometh, baffometi, Occitan Bafometz) is an imagined pagan deity (i.e., a product of xtian folklore concerning pagans), revived in the 19th century as a figure of occultism and Satanism. It first appeared in 11th and 12th century Latin and Provençal as a corruption of "Mahomet", the Latinisation of "Muhammad", but later it appeared as a term for a pagan idol in trial transcripts of the Inquisition of the Knights Templar in the early 14th century. The name first came into popular English-speaking consciousness in the 19th century, with debate and speculation on the reasons for the suppression of the Templars.

Black Magic - Magic involving the supposed invocation of evil spirits or demons for evil purposes.

Black Mass - Ritual of the church of Satan; performed to blaspheme and free the participants from the hold of anything widely accepted as sacred, not just organized religion, as in the traditional Black Mass which is meant as a blasphemy against Catholicism. (aka Messe Noire)

Caveat Emptor - The principle that the buyer alone is responsible for checking the quality and suitability of goods before a purchase is made.

Chakra - Chakra are believed to be centers of the body from which a person can collect energy. They are connected to major organs or glands that govern other body parts.

Chalice - A chalice (from Latin calix, cup, borrowed from Greek kalyx, shell, husk) is a goblet or footed cup intended to hold a drink. In general religious terms, it is intended for drinking during a ceremony.

Coitus Interruptus - Also known as the rejected sexual intercourse, withdrawal or pullout method, is a method of birth-control in which a man, during intercourse withdraws his penis from a woman's vagina prior to ejaculation. The man then directs his ejaculate (semen) away from his partner's vagina to avoid insemination.

Concubine - Concubinage is an interpersonal relationship in which a person engages in an ongoing relationship (usually matrimonially oriented) with another person to whom they are not or cannot be married; the inability to marry is usually due to a difference in social status or economic condition. Historically, the relationship involved a man in a higher status position, usually with a legally sanctioned spouse, who maintains a second household with the lesser "spouse". The woman in such a relationship is referred to as a concubine.

Conjure - To make (something) appear unexpectedly or seemingly from nowhere as by magic.

Coven - A group or gathering of witches or Satanists who meet regularly.

Crone - High ranking member of a Satanic coven. Assists and advises the coven High Priestess on magic, ritual and coven historical accounts.

Demonology - The study of demons or of demonic belief.

Divine Comedy - The Divine Comedy (Italian: Divina Commedia) is an epic poem written by Dante Alighieri between 1308 and his death in 1321.

It is widely considered the preeminent work of Italian literature, and is seen as one of the greatest works of world literature. The poem's imaginative and allegorical vision of the afterlife is a culmination of the medieval world-view as it had developed in the Western Church. It helped establish the Tuscan dialect, in which it is written, as the standardized Italian language. It is divided into three parts: Inferno, Purgatorio, and Paradiso.

Evocation - The act of calling or summoning a spirit, demon, god or other supernatural agent, in the Western mystery tradition. Comparable practices exist in many religions and magical traditions and may use potions with and without uttered word formulas.

Fasching - The German carnival season.

Grimoire - A Grimoire is a description of a set of magical symbols / actions and how to combine them properly.

Habit (cloth) - A long, loose garment worn by a member of a religious order or congregation.

Hell - A place regarded in various religions as a spiritual realm of evil and suffering, often traditionally depicted as a place of perpetual fire beneath the earth where the wicked are punished after death.

Higher Magic - Higher order of cognitive and magical abilities.

Incantation - A series of words said as a magic spell.

Incubus - A male demon that has sexual intercourse with sleeping women.

Inner Sanctum - The most sacred place of magical workings for a coven.

Inverted Pentagram - A five-pointed star that is formed by drawing a continuous line in five straight segments, often used as a mystic and magical symbol. Often used by occult practitioners.

Invocation - The action of invoking something or someone for assistance or as an authority. An invocation (from the Latin verb invocare "to call on, invoke, to give") may take the form of:

Supplication, prayer or spell.

A form of possession.

Command or conjuration.

Self-identification with certain spirits.

Lex Talionis - Law of the jungle or the talon. The natural order where the weak are allowed to perish, the strong survive. Darwin's survival of the fittest.

LHP - Left-Hand Path, is a term used in the Western esotericism.

Loup-garou - A person cursed to live as a Lycanthrope. (aka werewolf).

Messe Noire - See Black Mass.

Nostradamus - Michel de Nostredame, usually Latinised as Nostradamus, was a French apothecary and reputed seer who published collections of prophecies that have since become famous worldwide. He is best known for his book Les Propheties (The Prophecies), the first edition of which appeared in 1555. Since the publication of this book, which has rarely been out of print since his death, Nostradamus has attracted a following that, along with much of the popular press, credits him with predicting many major world events.

Orgasm - A climax of sexual excitement, characterized by feelings of pleasure centered in the genitals and (in men) experienced as an accompaniment to ejaculation.

Poser - Anarchists who hide behind Satanism to satisfy their own desires; not those of Satan.

Rite - A religious or other solemn ceremony or act.

Rituale Romanum - The Roman Ritual (Latin: Rituale Romanum) is one of the official ritual works of the Roman Rite of the Catholic Church. It contains all the services which may be performed by a priest or deacon which are not contained within either the Missale Romanum or the Brevarium Romanum. The book also contains some of the rites which are contained in only one of these books for convenience.

Samael - Samael (Hebrew: סמאל) (also Sammael and Samil) is an important archangel in Talmudic and post-Talmudic lore, a figure who is accuser, seducer and destroyer, and has been regarded as both good and evil.

Sex Magic - Sex magic is a term for various types of sexual activity used in magical, ritualistic, or otherwise religious and spiritual pursuits. One practice of sex magic is using the energy of sexual arousal or orgasm with visualization of a desired result. A premise of sex magic is the idea that sexual energy is a potent force that can be harnessed to transcend one's normally perceived reality. Oral, vaginal, anal and other methods are employed during sex magic rituals.

Shemhamforash - The Shemhamphorasch is a corruption of the Hebrew term Shem ha-Mephorash (שם המפורש), which was used in tannaitic times to refer to the Tetragrammaton. In early Kabbalah the term was used to designate sometimes a seventy-two Letter name for God, and sometimes a forty-two Letter name. Rashi said Shem ha-Mephorash was used for a forty-two letter name, but Maimonides thought Shem ha-Mephorash was used only for the four letter Tetragrammaton.

Sigil of Baphomet - The seal or image of Baphomet. Also see Baphomet.

Socratic Method - The Socratic method (also known as method of elenchus, elenctic method, Socratic irony, or Socratic debate), named after the classical Greek philosopher Socrates, is a form of inquiry and debate between individuals with opposing viewpoints based on asking and answering questions to stimulate critical thinking and to illuminate ideas. It is a dialectical method, often involving an oppositional discussion in which the defense of one point of view is pitted against the defense of another; one participant may lead another to contradict himself in some way, thus strengthening the inquirer's own point.

Succubus - A female demon believed to have sexual intercourse with sleeping men.

Satanic Bible - The Satanic Bible is a collection of essays, observations, and rituals published by Anton LaVey in 1969. It contains the core principles of the religion of LaVeyan Satanism, and is considered the foundation of its philosophy and dogma. It has been described as the most important document to influence contemporary LaVeyan Satanism. Though The Satanic Bible is not considered to be sacred scripture in the way the xtian bible is to xtianity, LaVeyan Satanists regard it as an authoritative text; it has been referred to as "quasi-scripture." It extols the virtues of exploring one's own nature and instincts. Believers have been described as "atheistic Satanists" because they believe that God is not an external entity, but rather something that each person creates as a projection of his or her own personality—a benevolent and stabilizing force in his or her life. At the time of printing of Sanctum of Shadows, there have been thirty printings of The Satanic Bible, through which it has sold over a million copies.

SWOT Analysis - A useful technique for understanding your Strengths and Weaknesses, and for identifying both the Opportunities open to you and the Threats you face.

Third Eye - The innate ability to sense and understand more than meets the eye.

Thurible - A thurible is a metal censer suspended from chains, in which incense is burned during worship services.

Thurifer - The person who carries the thurible.

Vampire - Those beings (undead or living creature) who survive by feeding on the blood of living creatures.

Wimple - A cloth headdress covering the head, the neck, and the sides of the face, formerly worn by women and still worn by some nuns.